THE MEDITATION WORKBOOK

160+ MEDITATION TECHNIQUES TO REDUCE
STRESS AND EXPAND YOUR MIND

AVENTURAS DE VIAJE

Illustrated by
LOUIE CAMILLE RODRIGUEZ

WARNINGS AND DISCLAIMERS

The information in this publication is made public for reference only.

Neither the author, publisher, nor anyone else involved in the production of this publication is responsible for how the reader uses the information or the result of his/her actions.

CONTENTS

THANKS FOR YOUR PURCHASE

Did you know you can get FREE chapters of any SF Nonfiction Book you want?

https://offers.SFNonfictionBooks.com/Free-Chapters

You will also be among the first to know of FREE review copies, discount offers, bonus content, and more.

Go to:

https://offers.SFNonfictionBooks.com/Free-Chapters

Thanks again for your support.

INTRODUCTION

Many people avoid meditation because they think it's difficult to practice or they don't have enough time. Don't let these things stop you. While you'll get more benefits the more you do, anything is better than nothing—and I mean anything. Even one minute a day is a great start.

Once you get over the initial "hump," I bet you will soon do 2 minutes, then 5, then 10+.

This book includes over 160 meditations from a variety of disciplines. Anyone with the slightest interest in meditation will find something they can use.

Can't sit still? Use a moving meditation.

Can't focus on breathing? Try visualization.

Don't have time? Incorporate meditation with exercise.

There are so many different ways to meditate in this book that you're bound to find at least one which resonates with you.

Benefits of Meditation

Almost all religions include meditation in some form (prayer, for example), and many non-religious people use meditation as a path towards enlightenment. But a spiritual awakening isn't the only benefit of meditation. Some meditations have specific healing purpose, and many people use them to achieve mental, emotional, and spiritual clarity.

Some specific benefits of meditation include:

- Building inner compassion
- Controlling anxiety

- Decreasing blood pressure
- Enhancing self-awareness
- Boosting general well-being
- Improving sleep
- Increasing focus
- Controlling pain
- Promoting emotional health
- Overcoming addiction
- Reducing memory loss
- Reducing stress

The meditations in this book can help you achieve any (or all) of these things.

Explaining Energy

Many meditations involve the harnessing and/or movement of energy through and beyond the body.

Different disciplines call this energy different things, but they are essentially the same. You may know it as qi (chi), prana, life force, ki, etc. Just know that when these are referenced in this book (whichever term), I am talking about the non-physical, essential energy of the universe.

As I said earlier, this energy is present throughout the universe, and the universe provides it in abundance for all. In living creatures, it flows through the body.

Categorizing Meditation

The way I categorized the meditations in this book is a little arbitrary. Most of them fall into multiple categories. I put each one in what I thought to be its primary category, but if you disagree with it, that's fine. It will not hinder you in doing any of the meditations.

There is a little introduction at the start of each section to give you a background on that meditation type.

Each of the meditation types are complete subjects on their own, and you could give any of them your full devotion. To get into the deep aspects of any type is not the aim of this book. Rather, it's to give an overview of all of them.

While doing the meditations in this book, you may find you prefer one type. That's great, and you can do deeper research into it if you want to achieve more.

I've done this myself. I prefer active meditations, and have further studied meditation in movement with yoga and martial arts. I also enjoy guided and metta meditations. These are just my personal preferences. Do as you feel.

BREATHING

Focusing on your breath is a well-known method of meditation, and is a good way to ease your body into a state of calm and relaxation. Most breathing meditations are mindfulness meditations.

Diaphragmic Breathing

This helps you to breathe from your diaphragm, as opposed to breathing shallowly as most people do. It's a good stress reliever.

1. Sit or lie down in a comfortable position.
2. Close your eyes and pay attention to your breath.
3. Notice the depth and speed at which you're breathing.
4. When you're ready, consciously alter your breathing so that it's deeper and slower.
5. Inhale the air all the way down into your diaphragm and exhale until you're empty.

Inflating the Balloon

If you have difficulty with the previous meditation, this one may help.

It combines diaphragmatic breathing with visualization.

1. Breathe in through your nose and out through your mouth.
2. Imagine your abdomen is a white balloon.
3. As you inhale, imagine the balloon filling up with positive energy (love, kindness, creativity, etc.).
4. As you exhale, the air escapes from the balloon, and the positive feelings spread throughout your entire being. You don't force the air out; it escapes on its own.

Alternate Nostril Breathing

Alternate nostril breathing is an easy way to pay attention to your breath. It calms the mind and raises awareness.

1. Sit in a comfortable position and place your right thumb on your right nostril.
2. Press your right nostril closed and inhale through your left nostril.
3. Next, release your thumb and close your left nostril with your pinky and fourth finger.
4. Exhale though your right nostril and then inhale through the same nostril.
5. Release your left nostril and close your right nostril. Inhale through your left nostril.
6. Repeat this pattern at whatever pace feels most relaxing for you.

Cleansing Breath

This is a good way to release tension and stress, especially from your shoulders.

1. Take a deep breath in through your nose. Inhale as much as you can without becoming distressed.
2. Exhale until your lungs are completely empty.
3. Repeat this to dissipate any tension.

Counted Breathing

Counting is a good way to keep focused on your breaths. It also allows you to elongate your breath.

1. Sit in a comfortable position.

2. Place your tongue right behind your teeth on the roof of your mouth.
3. Inhale through your nose as you count down from 5.
4. Exhale through your mouth as you count up to 8.
5. Feel your lungs empty completely as you relax into the breath.
6. Repeat this.

4-7-8 Breathing

This is a variation of the counted breathing meditation in which you pause between your breaths.

1. Sit in a comfortable position.
2. Place your tongue right behind your teeth on the roof of your mouth.
3. Inhale through your nose as you count to 4.
4. Wait at the top of your breath for a count of 7.
5. Exhale through your mouth as you count to 8.
6. Feel your lungs empty completely as you relax into the breath.
7. Repeat this.

The count of 4-7-8 is flexible. Use whatever breathing ratio feels best for you.

10 to 1

This is another variation of counting breaths. Your aim is to get all the way to the last number (1) without getting distracted.

1. Notice your breathing. Feel the air being drawn in and out.
2. As you inhale, mentally say "ten."
3. As you exhale, repeat the number in your mind.

4. On the next breath, mentally repeat "nine" on inhale and exhale.
5. Continue this pattern all the way to "one."
6. If you get distracted, start from ten again.

Objective Breathing

1. Sit in a comfortable position and focus on the movement of your breath.
2. As you breathe in and out, notice the air moving through you.
3. Continue to focus on your breath in this way for the entirety of your practice. If you get distracted, acknowledge it and refocus back on your breath.
4. Don't get lost in anything that arises.

Releasing Your Stress

1. Start with diaphragmatic breathing.
2. As you inhale, imagine all the stress in your body being drawn into your chest.
3. On your exhale, visualize all that stressful energy being expelled out through your breath.
4. Repeat this process.

Zazen

Zazen is a Japanese seated meditation. There are specific seated poses you can use, but sitting cross-legged on the floor is sufficient. The important thing is to keep your back straight.

1. Close your mouth and rest your gaze on the ground about a meter in front of you.
2. Press your tongue lightly on the roof of your mouth and

swallow once.

3. Release the tension from your body, but don't slouch.
4. Place your dominant hand over the other, with both palms facing up. The knuckles should overlap and your thumbs should touch lightly.
5. Rest your hands in your lap.
6. Focus on your breath moving in and out through your nose.
7. Center your focus on your breath and your hara (your spiritual center). Your hara is two inches below the navel inside your body.
8. When you're are ready, rock back and forth. Allow your rocking to get less and less pronounced until you settle in your center of gravity. As you do this, keep your attention on your hara and your breath.
9. Count your breaths. Each inhale and exhale is one count. Count from 10 to 1. That is:
10. Inhale: 10, Exhale: 9, Inhale: 8, etc.
11. When you get to 1, or whenever you get distracted, start from 10 again.
12. Let any arising thought pass. If it returns repeatedly, that's fine. Continue to let it pass through without judgement. Don't suppress any thoughts. Let them flow through.
13. When you can get to 10 repeatedly without getting distracted, count each cycle of breath. That is, treat the inhale and exhale as one count.
14. Eventually, you'll be able to abandon the counting. Your breath will flow on its own, and you'll flow with it. But don't rush going through these three breathing steps, or you'll get stuck in single-pointedness of mind (samadhi).

Related Chapters:

- Mindfulness
- Visualization

DAOIST

Daoism (Taoism) is a Chinese philosophy and religion with a focus on living in harmony with nature.

Daoist meditation focuses on the generation, transformation, and circulation of inner energy. With it, you quiet and unify the mind, body, and spirit. Some Daoist meditations focus on improving health and longevity.

Your Lower Dantian

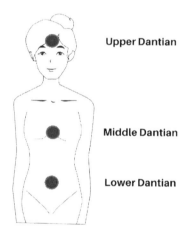

In Daoism, the energy centers in your body are your dantian.

There are three main dantian, but the most important is the lower one. It is the foundation of your internal energy (qi). In Japan, they call it your hara, and in yoga it is the swadhisthana chakra (the seat of prana).

Your lower dantian is where you focus your breathing during meditation. It's about three fingers below and two fingers behind your belly button.

The other two main dantian are the upper and middle dantian. The middle dantian is nourishment, and sits at heart level. Your upper dantian is your "third eye," and relates to forward vision in life.

Breath and Navel Meditation

This Daoist meditation is the oldest meditation on record in China and India, and is a good place for beginners to start. Use it to develop focused attention and single awareness.

When doing this meditation, focus on the natural flow of breath in your nostrils and the movement of your abdomen—that is, on expansion and contraction.

1. Sit in a comfortable position. Ensure you're well-balanced.
2. Have your mouth naturally closed and your eyes almost shut. Press your tongue to the roof of your mouth.
3. Take a long, smooth breath in through your nose, so it goes all the way into your abdomen.
4. As you inhale, focus on making your inhale like a gentle wind.
5. As you exhale, "follow" the air out as far as you can. It may even touch the floor.
6. You should also focus on the contraction of your abdomen. Notice the expansion and contraction of it with each breath you take.

If focusing on your nostrils and your abdomen simultaneously doesn't suit you, you can do one at a time, or alternate between them.

Another alternative is to count your breaths. This is a good way to start if you have trouble focusing.

Central Channel

This is a simple way to develop an awareness of qi in the body. The ideal time to do it is at dawn or midnight.

1. Sit in a comfortable position.
2. Take a deep breath in.
3. Bend forward slowly as you exhale through your mouth. Breathe out until your lungs are empty.
4. Do steps 2 and 3 another two times (three times in total). When you inhale, you come back to the seated position, and bend over again as you exhale.
5. After the third repetition, sit still and breathe naturally.
6. Imagine and focus on a beam of energy entering the crown of your head. In Daoism, this is the "medicine palace." You may know it better as the seventh chakra.
7. As you inhale, feel and follow this beam of energy flow in through your medicine palace and down through your body until it reaches your lower dantian.
8. As you exhale, follow the energy beam back up through your body and out your medicine palace.

Soon enough, you'll feel the energy at your crown at the beginning of the inhalation and the end of the exhalation, in the form of numbness, tingling, or warmth. After some practice, you will feel the energy moving through your body. At this stage, you can experiment with allowing the energy to exit at different points of your body. For example, you can try pushing it out through your third eye or the palms of your hands. Regardless of where you let the energy exit, always let it enter through the medicine palace.

If you tremble, rock, or have any other spontaneous movement, don't fight it, but don't encourage it either. This is your energy channels opening. Let the energy course through of its own accord.

Martial Walking

Daoist martial arts use walking exercises for martial development.

They are not like other walking meditations, since they focus more on the physical benefits, but they include some mental training.

Here is a video example:

https://www.youtube.com/watch?v=crXYjl1RLcY

Opening the Three Passes

This meditation circulates your qi around the body by activating your "microcosmic orbit." Activating your microcosmic orbit is vital before learning advanced Daoist meditation practices.

This is the best Daoist method for health, longevity, and starting on the path to a higher spiritual awareness.

1. Sit in a comfortable position, with your eyes almost shut, and regulate your breath.
2. Visualize a sphere of energy in your navel. At the center of it is a point of pure, clear, bright light. Allow it to glow into your umbilical region (lower dantian).
3. Feel your breath become lighter and lighter.
4. When you have a stable, subtle breath and the energy is full, visualize the energy traveling down to your perineum and back up through your coccyx. It continues to rise through your spine to the back of your brain. Breathe naturally.
5. Now imagine your "true spirit" in the center of your brain (the nirvana chamber) accepting all the energy. Aid this by moving your head forward and tilting it a little upward. Press your tongue on the roof of your mouth.
6. Your nirvana chamber might warm and/or feel swollen. This means the energy is in there.

7. Next, visualize the energy from your nirvana chamber coming out your third eye.
8. When you feel the center of your brows throb, it's a sign that your third eye is opening. Draw the energy out through the eye. Opening this pass will open all your energy passes. You may feel this through your entire body.
9. After a few minutes, allow the energy to sink down through the roof of your mouth, into your tongue, and down your throat into your heart. Do not swallow. Allow it to flow down on its own.
10. Now return the energy to the root. Do this by visualizing it traveling down from your heart through your solar-plexus, then navel, and into your lower dantian. It will soak through your internal organs and rest in your genitals.
11. Begin another cycle up through your body to the center of your brain, as previously described.
12. If you get to where you can complete a full energy cycle (a microcosmic orbit) in one breath, draw energy down as you inhale (from upper to lower dantian) and raise it up on your exhale.

If you tremble, rock, or have any other spontaneous movement, don't fight it, but don't encourage it either. This is your energy channels opening. Let the energy course through of its own accord.

Pulled by the Dantian

This exercise can be grounding and energizing, especially for those who rarely lead with their dantian.

1. Walk at your normal speed.
2. As you walk, focus your attention on your dantian and allow it to pull you forward.

Seated Qigong

Qigong isn't specifically Daoist, but Daoist meditators are high-level qigong achievers.

It is also present in other Chinese practices, such as traditional medicine, Buddhism, and martial arts.

I put this meditation here because it references the lower dantian.

1. Sit in a comfortable position, balanced and centered.
2. Relax your whole body and regulate your breathing. Make it long, deep, and easy.
3. Once your mind is calm, focus on your lower dantian, so that your qi will gather there.
4. Feel the qi circulating through your body.

Zhuanqi

This is a Daoist breathing meditation to "unite mind and qi." The aim is to "focus your vital breath until it is supremely soft."

1. Sit crossed legged on the ground, with your back straight.
2. Half-close your eyes while gazing at the tip of your nose.
3. Observe your breath.
4. Join your breath and your mind together. If this is too cryptic for you to begin with, start by focusing on your lower dantian.

Zuowang

Zuowang is the classic Daoist "emptiness" meditation. The goal is to empty your mind and "forget about everything." It is a simple premise, but difficult to achieve in practice.

1. Sit crossed legged on the ground, with your back straight.

2. Half-close your eyes while gazing at the tip of your nose.
3. Allow all thoughts and sensations to come and go. Don't engage any of them. Just let them flow through.
4. Join your breath and your mind together. If this is too cryptic for you to begin with, start by focusing on your lower abdomen.

Related Chapters:

- Breathing
- Gazing

GAZING

Gazing meditation is a method you can use to achieve stillness of the mind through your eyes.

Your eye movement patterns depend on your state of mind. For example, the micro-movements of your eyes are different if you're angry than if you're calm.

If you control your eye movement, you can influence your mental and emotional state. Stillness of eyes brings stillness of mind.

Other benefits of gazing include increasing focus, lower stress, eye health, and headache relief. Here are some gazing guidelines:

- Watch whatever object you choose carefully, but don't stare intensely.
- Gaze as if you're looking for something. Watch the object without thinking about it.
- Experiment with the intensity of your gaze. Make it soft or piercing, or something in between.
- Keep your focus without blinking and without your thoughts wandering. With practice, you'll be able to go for a longer time without blinking or losing focus.
- Don't strain your eyes. When you really need to blink, do so, but don't move your pupils.
- Relax your eyes as much as you can.
- Have the object at eye level.
- Be sure you can see the object in focus. Wear your eyeglasses if you need to.
- Unless instructed to have total darkness, have a dim light behind you.
- Keep some tissues close by to wipe your eyes.
- To avoid headaches, start with sessions of less than 10 minutes.

I encourage you to use the gazing mediations in this section to begin with. After that, you can do gazing with almost anything. Here are some ideas:

- A black dot on a white wall
- Any image with significance for you
- Your right eye in a mirror
- A needle
- Flowing water
- The moon
- A star

Boochari Mudra

This is a yoga gazing meditation.

1. Sit in a comfortable position and bring your hand in front of your face.
2. Gaze at the tip of your finger for a few minutes.
3. Continue to gaze at the same spot while you lower your hand. You are now gazing at where your fingertip used to be.
4. Only know the space and emptiness.
5. When you lose focus, start again.

Candle Gaze One

Gazing at a candle is a great place to start with this type of meditation. The flame is easy to focus on, and it leaves a clear after-image in your mind.

There are some cautions though:

- Don't practice candle gazing every day for more than six weeks. Some people believe it will leave a permanent impression on the retina. Swap to another object every so often.

- Don't do any candle gazing if you have astigmatism, cataracts, epilepsy, glaucoma, or myopia.

1. Light a candle in a room that's dark and still, where there's no breeze.
2. Sit a few feet away from the candle and gaze at the flame. Watch it carefully, but don't stare intensely.
3. Keep your eyes still.
4. After two minutes, close your eyes.
5. Look at the after-image that appears in your mind.
6. Play with that image however you wish. Imagine it still in the center, growing or shrinking, changing color, or getting brighter or dimmer.
7. When you're ready, open your eyes and gaze at the flame again.
8. After a few more minutes, close them again and play with the mental image.
9. Repeat this process for as long as you wish.

Candle Gaze Two

1. Light a candle in a room that's dark and still, where there's no breeze.
2. Sit a few feet away from the candle and gaze at the flame. Watch it carefully, but don't stare intensely.
3. Keep your eyes still.
4. Continue to gaze until your eyes tear.
5. Close your eyes, but keep gazing at the same point.
6. After 20 seconds, relax your eyes.
7. Cover your eyes with the palms of your hands. Do not put pressure on your eyeballs.

8. Gently move your palms in circles, and wipe your eyes if needed.
9. Repeat the practice.

Eyebrow Gazing

Eyebrow gazing will increase the expansion and alertness of your third eye.

1. Hold out a finger about 10 cm away from the point at the center of your eyebrows and level with it.
2. Gaze at the tip of your finger for a few minutes.
3. Once you're comfortable, bring your finger closer to the center of your eyebrows. Don't break your gaze. If you need to, you can pause along the way until your eyes adjust.
4. Once you touch the center of your eyebrows with your fingertip, drop your finger and gaze at that point.

Gazing in Darkness

These instructions are simple, but the meditation is powerful. It may trigger past traumatic experiences.

1. Sit or stand in a room where there is no light at all.
2. Gaze at a spot in front of you.

Gazing in Shared Space

1. Sit in a comfortable position.
2. Choose two objects you can see at the same time.
3. Focus on a space between them.
4. When you're ready, shut your eyes and focus on "the space between your thoughts."

Internal Image Gazing

Internal gazing is a when you gaze at a mental image of an object.

1. Sit in a comfortable position and close your eyes.
2. Focus your gaze on your third eye.
3. Steady your breath and your thoughts.
4. Pick one thought or picture in your mind to focus on, preferably something denoting love, like the image of a family member.
5. Gaze at the mental picture.
6. When you're ready, make your field of vision smaller until your focus is on one point in the picture.
7. Once you completely forget your surroundings, you'll be in deep meditation.

Internal Scenery Gazing

1. Sit in a comfortable position and close your eyes.
2. Focus your gaze on any point in front of you while observing the entire scene around you.
3. Close your eyes and fix your awareness on your third eye, while mentally recreating the scenery in your mind.

Kasina Gazing

In this Theravada Buddhism meditation there are 10 recommended objects for you to gaze at: earth, water, fire, wind, white, yellow, red, blue, space (or sky), and bright light.

1. Find an object in one of the categories above to meditate upon.
2. Sit or stand in a comfortable position and gaze at it.

3. When you're ready, close your eyes and gaze at the image of the object in your mind.
4. If you lose the image, open your eyes and start again.

You could also do this entirely in your mind, as internal image gazing.

Nose Tip Gazing

1. Hold out a finger about 10 cm away from the tip of your nose and level with it.
2. Gaze at the tip of your finger for a few minutes.
3. Once you're comfortable, bring your finger closer to your nose. Don't break your gaze. If you need to, you can pause along the way until your eyes adjust.
4. Once you touch your nose with your fingertip, drop your finger and gaze at your nose.

Sky-Gazing

This Tibetan Buddhism gazing method is more about resting the mind in a natural state than it is about concentration.

1. Find a spot where you can see nothing but the sky in your field of vision, either lying on your back or sitting somewhere high.
2. Get comfortable and take a few deep breaths to calm your mind.
3. Gaze into the sky.
4. Let all thoughts pass through your mind as it merges with the sky.

Zen Floor-Gazing

1. Sit in a comfortable position and gaze a few feet ahead of you into the ground.
2. Gaze softly.
3. When you're ready, bring your attention to your breath and body.
4. Just sit.

Zen Wall-Gazing

1. Stand facing a wall. A blank wall is easier to begin with.
2. Look at a point about the same height as your thigh.
3. Gaze though the wall, opening your peripheral vision.
4. When you're ready, bring your attention to your breath and body.
5. Just sit.

GUIDED

A guided meditation is when you listen to a recording or live speaker that/who guides you through the meditation.

The way you're guided depends on the type of meditation. You can find guided meditations based on almost all types of traditional meditation.

There are also guided meditations that only exist because of modern recording technology. Binaural Beats, for example, are recordings that stimulate your mind into generating alpha waves, which are the brainwaves associated with initial levels of meditation.

Here are a couple of links where you can download some free guided meditations. There are also plenty on YouTube.

https://www.uclahealth.org/marc/mindful-meditations

https://www.yogajournal.com/meditation/meditation-sounds-daily-life

https://www.binauralbeatsmeditation.com

LOVING KINDNESS

Loving kindness meditation (metta meditation) is a Buddhist Zazen meditation with a focus on compassion.

"Metta" is a Pali word which translates to kindness, benevolence, and good will. The benefits of metta meditation include an increase in positive emotions such as:

- Compassion
- Confidence
- Self-acceptance
- Empathy
- Purpose

Calm Heart Meditation

This meditation is a good way to cleanse your heart, especially when you feel emotionally drained or overwhelmed.

1. Sit in a comfortable position.
2. Touch the tips of your index fingers and thumbs together on both hands. Place your hands on your knees.
3. If you want to calm your mind, have your palms facing down. To open your awareness, face your palms up.
4. Straighten your back, but stay relaxed. Tilt your chin down to lengthen your neck.
5. Mentally scan your body from head to toe. Consciously release any tension you find as you go.
6. When you're ready, notice the center of your chest.
7. Repeat the mantra "om" on each exhalation, either silently or out loud.
8. With each exhale, feel the sound of "om" expanding your heart and washing away any negativity.

9. A specific emotion may surface. Explore it. Be open to the discovery of insight.

10. Your chanting of "om" will dissolve it. Continue your meditation as normal.

Healing Conflicts

This meditation is good for resolving any negative feelings you may have toward someone of importance to you, such as a family member, friend, or colleague. It will also help you develop a positive connection with all beings and dissipate your negative emotions.

1. Sit in a comfortable position with your eyes closed.

2. Think of the person you have a conflict with. Bring up an image of him or her in your mind.

3. Now, in your mind, be that person. Encompass all that person is, both negative and positive.

4. Start simple, by envisioning yourself wearing his/her clothes.

5. Delve in deeper, so that you have his/her dreams, difficulties, history, and future.

6. Notice how it feels to be the person. Understand him or her from within.

7. Now send love and kindness to the person.

8. Repeat the mantra "May you be happy. May you be safe. May you be at peace."

9. As you repeat the mantra, imagine a beam of loving light shooting out from your heart and embracing the person.

10. When you are ready, come out of the mediation.

11. Take a few moments to notice how your feelings about the person have changed.

Loving All

This meditation is a variation on the four stages of Patanjali's Yoga Sutra.

1. Sit in a comfortable position, with a straight spine and relaxed body. Rest your hands on your thighs.
2. Focus your attention on your breath.
3. Inhale deep into your abdomen while mentally saying "I am."
4. On your exhale, mentally say "calm and relaxed." Feel all your tension (physical and emotional) escape from your body.
5. Once you're relaxed and your mind is calm, focus on your heart. Feel each breath circulate around this area.
6. Notice any feelings or thoughts that arise, and let them pass without judgement.
7. After a few minutes, the excess feelings and thoughts will subside. At this stage, continue to focus your awareness on your heart while consciously changing your thought stream.
8. Cultivate an attitude of acceptance, compassion, and understanding with all beings.
9. Start with yourself, and then expand to your friends and people you know.
10. When you think of those who have done you wrong, forgive them in your heart and send them joy and kindness.
11. Open your heart wider, to all those that are suffering in the world. Send them your eternal love.
12. Finally, send feelings of general wellbeing and love to all beings in this world.
13. If at any time you are drawn to a specific person, such as a friend in pain, someone who inspires you, or even someone you don't get along with, that's fine. Follow your heart's desire to send positive energy to whoever it wants to go to.

Loving Kindness

1. Sit in a comfortable position and close your eyes.

2. Generate a feeling of love in your mind and heart. There are many ways you can do this, such as by:

- Repeating the mantra "May I be happy. May I be safe. May I be at peace."
- Visualizing a warm glowing orb of light around you.
- Remembering a time you felt truly loved by others, like your parents or your spouse.
- Doing a combination of the above.

3. Once you cultivate the feeling of loving kindness in yourself, you can progressively spread it out to the world.

- Yourself
- A good friend
- A neutral person
- A difficult person
- All four of the above equally

4. Continue to widen your circle of inclusion, until eventually you send the feeling out to the whole universe.

At the start, it's easiest to send the energy to people you know and/or those in proximity. You can try this progression:

- Household
- Family (including your extended one)
- Friends
- Your street (including strangers)
- Neighborhood
- City
- State
- Country
- Continent
- The world
- Our galaxy
- The universe

Loving-Kindness Walking

This combines loving kindness meditation with walking.

1. Walk slowly up and down on the same path.
2. With each step focus your feelings of loving kindness.
3. Mentally repeat the mantra "May all beings be happy, may all beings be at peace, may all beings be free from all suffering."

An alternative mantra to use is "May I be happy, may I be at peace, may I be free from all suffering."

Self-Love

1. Sit in a comfortable position with your eyes closed.
2. Recall a time when you felt deeply loved by someone, such as a family member.
3. Feel it deep inside. In your body, mind, and heart. Really connect with this feeling of love.
4. Place your hands on the middle of your chest repeat the mantra "May I be happy. May I be safe. May I be at peace."
5. As you say the mantra, feel a light full of love spreading from your chest throughout your whole body.

MINDFULNESS

"Mindfulness" is the common translation for the Buddhist term "sati." It is focusing on the present moment. When you practice it, you notice any emotions, sensations, or thoughts that arise and let them pass though without judgment.

Traditionally, mindfulness meditation uses the breath to stay present (see the Breathing chapter), but there are many variations. In fact, you can make almost any daily activity a method of mindfulness. Simply pay attention to the present moment and be aware of what you're doing instead of being on "automatic."

This book has quite a few examples. Once you give a few of them a go, I'm sure you'll understand how you can adapt mindfulness to your common daily activities.

Aromatherapy Meditation

For this meditation, you need a stick of incense. You'll practice mindfulness by focusing your attention on the smoke. You'll also get the side benefits of aromatherapy. If you are sensitive to smoke and/or have respiratory problems, skip this meditation.

1. Light some incense and sit in a comfortable position in front of it. Don't sit so close that you're inhaling the smoke.
2. Watch the movement of the smoke.
3. Immerse yourself in the patterns and swirls it makes.
4. If your mind wanders, bring your attention back to the smoke.

Bathtub Meditation

This combines a relaxing hot bath with meditation.

1. Run a hot bath at a temperature you can relax in. Add some aromatherapy products if you wish, and/or play some soothing music in the background.
2. Get in the bath and take a few minutes to get comfortable and relax.
3. Concentrate on your breath. Make it slow and deep, so it goes all the way to your stomach.
4. Next, turn your attention to your senses. Notice the temperature of the water, the smell of the soaps, the sound of the music, etc.
5. If your mind wanders to the past or future, acknowledge it and return to your present sensory experience.

Cleaning House

A clean space is a clean mind, and you can complement the act of cleaning with mindfulness.

1. Before you clean, have a positive frame of mind about it. It's not some menial chore. It's a means of stress relief and a pathway to understanding the self.
2. As you clean, focus on the exact thing you're doing, and nothing else.
3. Notice all the feelings and sensations. Engage all your senses. For example, note:

- The vibrations of the vacuum cleaner and the sound of the dirt being sucked up in the tube
- The warmth of clothing fresh from the dryer
- The smell of lemon-fresh cleaners
- The change of color from dirty to clean
- The sound of the water running and how it feels on your hands.

Cooking

Cooking is a great time to be mindful as it engages all of your senses.

1. See all the colors.
2. Feel all the textures.
3. Listen to the sounds of cutting, sizzling, etc.
4. Smell the flavorful aromas.
5. Taste your creation.

You can continue into mindful eating once your dish is complete.

Eating

Eating is something many people enjoy. With mindfulness, you take that pleasure to a new level.

This is also a good way to lose weight, as you will eat much slower than normal. Eating slower gives your mind more time to register fullness.

1. Choose a single morsel of food, such as a piece of fruit.
2. Pick it up and observe it fully: its temperature, texture, color, shape, density, etc.
3. Close your eyes and smell it. Take in all the aromas.
4. Now place it in your mouth. Feel it on your tongue and taste it before chewing.
5. When you're ready, bite into it. Notice any texture and flavor changes that happen as you bite. Feel it on your teeth.
6. Now swallow it. Feel it go down your throat.

Chocolate Meditation

This is a mindful eating exercise using chocolate. You will experience it with all your senses.

1. Get a bite-sized piece of chocolate. Dark chocolate works best, as it has stronger aromas and textures.
2. Sit in a comfortable position and take a few breaths to relax your body.
3. Close your eyes and smell the chocolate. Smell it deeply. Be one with the aroma.
4. Now open your eyes and look at it. See all the small details.
5. Take a small nibble. Let it sit on your tongue as you experience the flavor.
6. When you're ready, swallow it. Feel it go down your throat.
7. Notice the difference in your mouth before and after swallowing.
8. Now take another bite. As you raise the chocolate to your mouth, notice how it feels in your fingers.
9. Once it's in your mouth, experience the sensations of its flavor and texture once again.
10. If your mind wanders, acknowledge the distraction and then return your attention to the sensations the chocolate gives.

Drinking

You can also practice mindfulness with any drink.

1. Close your eyes and drink slowly.
2. Feel the temperature of the liquid as it goes over your tongue and down your throat.
3. Take the time to taste it fully.

Energy Massage

Many people love to get a massage, but you can receive just as much pleasure by giving one. It is also an effective way to create an energy connection with someone.

1. Learn some basic massage strokes. You can look them up on YouTube.
2. As you touch the receiver, focus deeply on your movement and the feel of his/her skin.
3. Feel the blood pulse through his/her body and into your hands. After a while, you may feel your pulses align.
4. Send feelings of love and kindness through your touch. It may help to imagine white or colored energy flowing from your heart through your hands and into the receiver.

Labeling Thoughts

Labeling your thoughts is especially useful when you want to change habitual thought patterns—to become more optimistic, for example. This is because it raises your awareness of what you think about.

1. Begin by being mindful of your breath using any breathing meditation.
2. When you're ready, open your awareness to your mind. Observe the feelings, images, thoughts, and words that pop up.
3. Label each thought that pops up, but don't dwell on it or make any judgement about it. It's neither positive nor negative. It's only a thought.
4. Once you have labeled the thought, let it pass through and move onto the next thought.

There are a few ways you can label your thoughts:

- Saying the label to yourself
- Visualizing it written
- Categorizing the thoughts as useful or not useful
- Classifying their function: fear, judgement, memory, planning, sensation, etc.

Mindful Walking

This meditation melds modern mindfulness with the traditional Buddhist walking meditation.

With it, you focus your attention on the sensations and perceptions of the present moment.

1. As you walk, pay attention to the full experience of walking.
2. Notice the ground touching your feet.
3. Notice each step your take in its entirety: the beginning, middle, and end.
4. Feel the muscles in your legs moving and the constant rebalancing of your body.
5. Scan your entire body, from your feet up. Notice any sensations as you walk.
6. If you feel any stiffness or pain in your muscles, consciously relax them.
7. Now notice your emotional and mental state. Balance and calm your mind with deep breathing if needed.
8. Finally, open your senses to the world around you—its sights, sounds, temperature, etc.

Music

The next time you listen to music, close your eyes and really listen to it.

1. Try to hear every part of a song, including each instrument (vocals are also an instrument).
2. Feel the vibrations of the music move through your body.
3. You can also sing or hum along.

Observing Thoughts

Observing thoughts is like labeling thoughts, but without the labeling. If you find this meditation difficult, start with labeling thoughts.

1. Begin by being mindful of your breath using any breathing meditation.
2. When you're ready, open your awareness to your mind. Observe the feelings, images, thoughts, and words that pop up.
3. Don't dwell on any single thought. They are neither good nor bad. They just are.
4. Allow each thought to pass through your mind like a floating twig in a stream, or a cloud in the sky being pushed away by a gentle breeze.

Samu Work

This is a Buddhist Zen practice. With it, you can meditate while doing any daily activity that doesn't require your full attention.

1. Do any activity at half speed or slower.
2. Use the extra time to be mindful and focus on your thoughts.

Shower Meditation

Instead of thinking what you did before or will do after the shower, use it to engage your senses in the present.

1. See the way the drops of water splash on the ground.
2. Feel the warm water stream over your skin.
3. Smell the fragrance of the soap.
4. Hear the running water.
5. Taste the water in your mouth.

Writing

Spontaneous writing is a good way to heal from traumatic events, but you can also use it to meditate. It's best to do this first thing in the morning, to clear out your mind before the day ahead.

1. Decide how much or how long you will write—one page or three minutes, for example.
2. Start writing and don't stop until you hit your length or time target. As you write, be very mindful of what you are doing.
3. Notice the feel of the pen or pencil on the paper.
4. Hear the scratching sound as you write.
5. Notice the way the imprint gets left on the paper.
6. If you run out of things to write, take a deep breath and start again.

The more you do this exercise, the deeper you'll go.

It may help to choose a subject to get you started, but don't feel the need to stick to it. You're free to write anything. It's the mindfulness that's important, not what you write.

Related Chapters:

- Breathing

MOVING

Movement meditation is a great way for those who can't sit still to meditate. You can settle a restless mind with movement meditation at any time of day. It works well for people because when the body is moving, it's easier to be mindful of its actions and sensations.

Centering Breath

This movement meditation takes its roots from the classic yoga sun salutation (surya namaskar).

You synchronize your movement and breath and then, as your breath slows, so does your movement. This returns balance to your inner self.

You can do this simple movement meditation seated or standing.

1. Bring your hands together at your heart.
2. Mentally scan your body and mind and ask yourself how you're feeling.
3. Notice your answer without analysis or judgement.
4. When you're ready, inhale through your nose as you bring your hands up.
5. Your breath and movement should be in sync. Your hands should come together over your head at the top of your inhalation.
6. As you exhale, bring your arms down the center of your body.
7. At the end of your exhalation, your arms should be resting beside your hips.
8. Repeat this movement and breathing. Focus on synchronizing the two.
9. When you feel the natural urge to finish your practice, do

one last cycle of your arms with your breath until your hands rest at your heart.

10. Stay in this position of quiet contemplation until you're ready to go on with your day.

Dancing Warrior

This dancing warrior sequence is from Vinyasa yoga. Take two or three breaths while in each pose.

1. Begin in downward dog.
2. Step your right foot forward and raise your hands into warrior I.
3. Go into warrior II by placing your right hand on the ground next to your right foot. Your left hand and foot should be in a straight line.
4. Next is reverse warrior. Straighten your torso and extend your arms out to your sides.
5. Finish with side angle pose by sliding your left hand down your calf.
6. Windmill your hands to the mat as you step back with your right foot, and go back into downward dog.
7. Repeat the sequence on your other side by stepping forward with your left foot.

Drawing

Drawing is a great way to engage with yourself creatively. If you don't want to just draw, you can try the following meditative exercise.

1. Find a black-and-white line drawing that you aren't familiar with.
2. Turn it upside down and then cover the picture so you can only see the bottom 5 centimeters.
3. On a separate piece of paper, draw exactly what you see.
4. Now uncover the next 5 centimeters and continue your drawing.
5. Continue to do this until you complete your drawing.

Hand Movement

In this exercise, you focus on moving your hands slowly and mindfully.

1. Sit comfortably. Deepen your breath and shake out your hands.
2. Place your hands on your thighs, palms up.
3. Focus on your hands. Try to feel your pulse in them.
4. Feel the air around them and around each finger.
5. Lift your hands up slowly. As soon as they are in the air, stop. Let them be still as you relax your shoulders, arms, and palms.
6. Continue to lift them as slowly as possible. Try make the movement so slow that your hands feel as if they're moving by themselves.
7. Imagine the molecules of air between your fingers.
8. When it feels right, face your palms inward and bring your hands together slowly.
9. As they get closer, feel them pulsing. Feel the energy between them.
10. Place your energetic hands anywhere on your body that needs healing.
11. Finish by letting your hands rest in your lap for a few minutes.

Hiking

Hiking is a great way to get closer to nature, and there are many ways to practice mindfulness while doing it.

1. Notice the color and shape of each flower.
2. Smell the foliage.
3. Feel the fresh air on your skin in as you breathe in.
4. Hear the sounds of the wilderness—the rustle of the leaves, the birds chirping, the insects crawling.
5. Feel your legs pumping as you hike.

Kundalini

Kundalini is meditation through dance. But you don't have to stop at a dance. Making noise and jumping around is a great way to connect your body and spirit. It naturally focuses your attention on motions and emotions, as opposed to thoughts.

With Kundalini meditation, you let go of ego and allow yourself to get lost in rhythm and movement.

Before you start, prepare some rhythmic instrumental music. It's important that the music not have any lyrics. The words will engage your thoughts, which is contrary to your aim.

1. Stand still, with your eyes closed. Breath slowly through your nose. Do this for a few minutes to calm your mind.
2. When you're ready, break into a dance. Move however you want to do so. Be expressive. Exaggerate your movements and vocalize if you like.
3. Let the movement and rhythm carry you to a higher state.
4. When you're finished with dancing, lie down and close your eyes.
5. Stay still for as long as you wish.

Martial Arts

Most traditional martial arts incorporate meditation, but you can also use the martial arts movements themselves as meditation. Tai chi is a great example of this, but various katas and drills from any style are a good form of meditation when used with mindfulness.

As you do the movements, focus on your breath and body movements. Let all other thoughts pass by. Be immersed in your practice.

Moving Qigong

Qigong often uses slow, rhythmic movement to improve and regulate your qi (life energy), though there are also still Qigong meditations. There are thousands of Qigong exercises. Here's a basic one.

1. Stand relaxed, with your feet shoulder-width apart and your knees a little bent.
2. Breathe naturally and notice how you feel.
3. When you're ready, inhale as you bring your arms level with your shoulders and slightly back. Your elbows should be bent and your fingers should point toward the sky.
4. Arch your spine a little as you open your chest and expand your ribcage.
5. Let your jaw go loose as your head drops backward.
6. Now, as you exhale, round your spine as if you're curling into a ball.
7. Draw your elbows together in front of your chest.
8. Allow your chin to drop to your chest.
9. Repeat this nine times, and finish standing straight and relaxed. This is one cycle.
10. Stay still and silent until you're ready to do another cycle.

Running

Reaching a state of meditative consciousness while running is commonly referred to as a runner's high. Turning your daily jog into a moving mindful meditation is easy. As you're running, focus your attention on a specific sensation, such as:

- Your breathing
- The cool breeze on your skin
- The sound of your feet hitting the ground

When ready, expand your awareness to the world around you. Choose specific sights, sounds, or smells to focus on.

Stretching

Stretching is a well-known way to relax the body. But this isn't yoga. With this stretching meditation, there's no need to follow specific sequences.

1. Find a quiet place with enough room for you to stretch. You can play some soothing music.
2. Start from the top of your body and work your way down, stretching each part.
3. As you do the stretches, pay attention to your breath.
4. Notice how your body feels as you stretch. Flow with the stretches.
5. After you have stretched each part of your body, from your head to your toes, lie on your back with your eyes closed.
6. Stay there for a few minutes and feel your body, stretched and relaxed.
7. When you are ready, get up slowly and go about your day.

Tai Chi

Tai chi is a Chinese moving meditation. It aligns the energy (qi) in your mind and body. If you do the tai chi movements quickly, it's akin to martial arts.

To use tai chi as meditation, move slowly. Focus on breathing and mindfulness.

When you first learn tai chi, you imitate the gross motions. As you get better, you learn more subtle movements as you align breath and motion. Eventually, you'll still your mind and feel the qi flow through you.

Describing how to do tai chi in words isn't practical, but here's a video you can watch and copy.

https://www.youtube.com/watch?v=ejB-jBtZqqU

Yoga Asanas

Yoga Asana sequences are the classic form of stretching yoga, which is a great form of exercise and a path to self-realization.

As in most moving meditations, you unite your breath and movements to achieve a meditative state.

When you first learn yoga, you imitate the poses as you align breath and motion. The more you practice, the more you learn, and the stronger your body gets. You can seek perfection in the poses as you still your mind and feel the prana flow through you.

Here's a link to a basic all-body yoga stretch routine:

https://www.survivalfitnessplan.com/beginner-yoga-for-flexibility-strength

Related Chapters:

- Breathing
- Mindfulness

WALKING MEDITATIONS

Walking meditation is a classic moving meditation.

There are many variations on how to do it, but in general, it's a very slow walk combined with coordinated breathing or other mindfulness techniques.

Before we get into all the variations of walking meditation, here are some general guidelines.

1. Choose somewhere you feel safe. Pick a spot that isn't crowded or polluted. Your backyard is a good place to start.
2. Fifteen minutes or longer is a good length of practice.
3. Move slowly and steadily. The slower you walk, the easier it is to stay in the present moment while stepping.
4. Before you walk, take a few minutes to stand still and balanced while breathing deeply. This anchors your attention to your body. You can do a full-body scan from your feet up.
5. If your mind wanders, acknowledge the thought and let it pass. Bring your attention back to your walking and breathing.
6. If you get drowsy, activate your mind by quietly reciting a mantra to yourself, and/or speed up your walk.

Ball of Energy

With this technique, you combine counted breathing and visualization with walking.

1. Walk at a slower pace than normal.
2. Inhale for 3, 6, or 12 paces.
3. Exhale for the same number of paces.

4. Once you're used to the rhythm, start visualizing qi flowing in and out through your breath.
5. Breathe all the qi that surrounds your body into your lower dantian (just below and behind your belly button).
6. As you breathe out, the qi in your dantian will expand into a ball around you.

You can hold your breath for the same number of paces in between steps 2 and 3.

Chankramanam

With this walking meditation, you synchronize the mental repetition of a mantra with your steps.

The number of steps you take to say the mantra is your choice. A short mantra may only take one or two steps, while a longer one may take several. Whatever you choose, be consistent. So, if you decide to say the mantra over two steps, always say that mantra over two steps.

1. Stand still and regulate your breath to calm yourself.
2. Repeat your mantra while standing.
3. Once you're ready, walk, while continuing to repeat your mantra.

Counting Steps

This variation of the walking meditation is good for those that get distracted easily. It will help to focus your mind.

1. Walk at a normal pace.
2. On your first step, mentally count the number "one."
3. On steps 2 and 3, mentally count "one, two."
4. On the next three steps, count "one, two, three."

5. Continue the pattern until you're counting "ten."

6. Once you reach "ten," start again, this time from "ten," and work your way down to "one." Your first step will be "ten," steps 2 and 3 will be "ten, nine," and so on.

Kinhin

Kinhin is walking meditation in Japanese Zen. You can do it on its own or between sessions of seated meditation. It has a very slow pace.

To do it, walk around the room in a clockwise direction.

1. Stand straight, but not stiff.
2. Let your weight balance evenly over your feet.
3. Notice your feet on the ground.
4. Create a relaxed fist, with your left hand around your left thumb, and position it just above your belly button.
5. Wrap your right hand around your left hand with your right thumb on top, resting in the crevice. This is shashu.
6. Look toward the ground about 1.5 meters in front of you, but don't focus.
7. Take a small step with your right foot. The step should be about the same length as your foot and last the same time as one complete breath (an inhale and an exhale).
8. Now do the same with your left foot.
9. Continue to take these small steps at this slow pace.
10. Keep your focus on your walking and breathing.

Pranayama Walking Meditation

Walking meditations are not as popular in yoga as it is in the Buddhist traditions, but there is this one. It involves coordinating breathing with stepping. With it, you actively guide your breath as opposed to merely observing it.

1. Stand still and breathe deeply until your mind, body, and breath are calm.
2. Start the breathing pattern of your choice while remaining still.
3. When you're ready, start taking steps. Each step should take one second.
4. Inhale, hold, and exhale for the required number of steps depending on the pattern you choose.

Suggested breathing patterns:

4-4-4-4

- Inhale over four steps.
- Hold your breath over four steps.
- Exhale over four steps.
- Hold your empty breath for four steps.

Increase or decrease the number of steps for each phase as you wish. For example, try a 3-3-3-3 or 5-5-5-5 pattern.

1-4-2

- Inhale over one step.
- Hold your breath over four steps.
- Exhale over two steps.

You can use a similar pattern with various tempos, such as 2-8-4 (doubled) or 3-12-6 (tripled).

Theravada Walking Meditation

This is the traditional Theravada Buddhist walking meditation. It involves more mental concentration than most other walking meditations in this book. With it, you will dedicate your attention to the feelings of walking and let go of everything else.

1. Choose a flat, straight path around 10 meters long, free from obstructions.

2. Stand straight and look down about 1.5 meters in front of you. Don't focus your sight on the ground. It may help to half-close your eyes.

3. Walk slowly, and notice the sensations you feel on the soles of your feet as they lift and land.

4. Notice the muscles in your legs and feet contract as you walk.

5. Feel the movement of your leg at it cuts through the air.

6. With each new step, old feelings will pass and new ones arise. Be mindful of these feelings.

7. Notice the six components of walking: raising, lifting, pushing, dropping, touching, and pressing. Mentally note them as they happen.

8. When you reach the end of the path, come to a complete stop. Take this moment of stillness as an opportunity to refocus your awareness if it has strayed. Do this every time you reach the end of the path.

9. Turn around and continue the walking meditation.

10. You can experiment with the speed. In time, you'll know which pace is best for you.

11. When your mind gets into a deep meditative state, you may enjoy standing still or sitting.

Thich Nhat Hanh's Walking Meditation

Thich Nhat Hanh (a Vietnamese monk) created a simplified version of walking meditation which uses affirmations.

1. Walk slowly and use deep breathing to calm yourself.

2. Notice each step and movement as they happen.

3. With each step, pass gratitude from your loving energy into the earth.

4. As you inhale, repeat to yourself, "I have arrived."

5. As you exhale repeat to yourself "I am home."
6. Continually repeat these affirmations and the sending of love to the earth.

You can use any affirmation you want. Here are more examples:

- Inhaling: "In the here." Exhaling: "In the now."
- Inhaling: "I am solid." Exhaling: "I am free."
- Inhaling: "In the ultimate." Exhaling: "I dwell."

Walking Beats

This walking meditation is good for those, like kids, who are too energetic to go for a slow pace.

1. Get yourself a metronome, or download an app for your phone.
2. Set the beat to 150 bpm (beats per minute).
3. On each beat, take a step.
4. After a minute, slow the beat down a little and step at the new pace.
5. Continue to slow the tempo until you get to 30 bpm.
6. Now you're walking at a calm pace. Synchronize your breathing with each step. Inhale for two steps, then exhale for two steps.

Wu Wei

Wu Wei (aimless walking) focuses on non-doing. In it, you move without purpose. Have no conscious mental effort. Be aimless.

1. Find an area where there is no need to pay attention to your surroundings. A circular or very long and straight path is best, to minimize the need to change direction.

2. To begin with, notice everything. Get comfortable with your surroundings.
3. Now ignore everything as you walk at a leisurely pace.

Related Chapters:

- Breathing
- Mindfulness
- Moving
- Visualization
- Mantras

SELF-AWARENESS

With these meditations, you'll focus your awareness within and connect with your true self. You'll learn to notice your thoughts, feelings, physical sensations, and more.

Five Inquiries

Contemplating these five inquiries will deepen your sense of well-being. Take the time experience each inquiry before moving on to the next.

1. Sit or lie down in a comfortable position.
2. Notice your senses interacting with your surroundings. Spend a few moments with each one (that is, with sight, sound, taste, touch, and smell).
3. Next, feel all your senses as one, and your whole being as a vibrant energy. Enjoy the feeling of "being."
4. When you're ready, contemplate each of the following inquiries.

Inquiry One: Where is "being" located?

Contemplate whether "being" has a physical boundary and/or a center point. Attempt to feel present in your body, yet beyond constraint at the same time.

Inquiry Two: Does "being" experience time?

In a state of being, your mind becomes calm and thoughts slow down to a halt. If there is no process of thought, is time passing by?

Inquiry Three: Can you improve "being"?

In a state of being, you are at one with yourself and the universe. You are as perfect as possible in that state and moment. Your core self wants for nothing regardless of what your physical mind and/or body wants.

Inquiry Four: Is "being" a familiar state?

Achieving a state of being is a feeling that everyone knows. You are comfortable in this state like you always have been, even if you can't remember when.

Inquiry Five: Is "being" complete?

After contemplating the five inquiries, rest with your mind still in the state of "being." You are spacious, beyond time, perfect, connected, and complete.

Before ending your practice, affirm your intention to experience this feeling of "being" as you go about your daily life. After some practice, resting in a state of undistracted "being" brings a sense of wholeness. You're complete just the way you are.

Aching Body Meditation

This is a good way to shift the way your mind experiences physical discomfort. It's not about making the pain disappear, but about exploring the truth of the sensation.

1. Sit or lie in a comfortable position, with your eyes closed. Be relaxed, but alert.
2. Take a few minutes to experience an awareness of your body.
3. Move your attention from your head to your toes and consciously relax any tense areas you encounter as you do so.
4. As you work your way down, notice anywhere your body contacts the floor.
5. Next, notice your whole body. Notice your heartbeat, the sensations on your skin, the movement of your chest and

abdomen as you breathe, and any other general sensations you feel.

6. Make a mental note of the sensations that stand out to you the most. Direct your attention to the area of your body that gives you the most intense sensation.

7. Trace the edges of the discomfort with your mind, as if you were tracing a picture.

8. Notice the various sensations at the edges of the area you traced. Perhaps there is movement, pressure, warmth, etc.

9. Now turn your attention to the sensations in your body outside of the traced area.

10. After a few minutes, return your attention to the traced area. Focus on the center of the pain and ask "what is this?" Notice everything about it (aching, throbbing, tightness, etc.).

11. When this becomes too intense, move your focus out of the traced area until calmness returns, then go back to it.

12. If there are several pain points, move your attention from one to the next.

13. When you finish, return your awareness to your whole body and rest a few minutes before continuing your day.

Feeling of Being

The feeling of "being" is natural, but with your busy life, you may neglect to experience it.

Taking the time to enjoy the feeling of "being" brings many positive, loving, and grounding feelings.

1. Scan your body from head to toe, consciously relaxing each body part as you go.

2. Keep your attention on the rise and fall of your abdomen with each breath you take.

3. Notice how and where you experience "being"— as a warmth in your heart, or a fuzziness in your belly, for example.

4. Keep your focus on these sensations as you read the following words for describing your experience of being. Take note if any stand out to you.

- Calm
- Connected
- Grounded
- Loving
- Peaceful
- Secure
- Spacious
- Well-being

5. When you come out of this meditation, write words that describe your own sense of being.

Meditating on the Ordinary

1. Sit or lie in a comfortable position and close your eyes.
2. Notice your breathing for a few moments to calm your mind.
3. Next, scan your body from head to toe. Notice any sensations you feel and your involuntary response to them.
4. When you get to a body part that has no sensations, rest your mind on it for a while.
5. Be curious about these "ordinary" body parts. How can you see them differently?
6. When you are ready, widen your field of awareness to the surrounding sounds.
7. Notice how you feel about each sound. Which are pleasant or unpleasant?
8. Indulge in the ordinary sounds, the ones like wind, traffic, or a ticking clock that are so common where you are that your mind usually disregards them.

9. Next, notice your thoughts. Allow each of them to pass through without your judgement.
10. Finally, allow yourself to take in every part of the present moment including all your senses and thoughts. Receive them all, but don't dwell on any.

Seer

1. Sit in a comfortable position with your eyes closed.
2. Gaze into the nothing in front of you.
3. When you're ready, reverse your gaze back towards yourself.
4. Gaze into yourself, into the "I."

Self-Inquiry

In this meditation, you'll endeavor to answer the question "Who am I?" beyond your egotistical self. The explanation of this is philosophical, but once you "get it," the practice is simple.

With self-inquiry, you ask yourself "Who am I?", but you don't seek tangible answers. Instead, you use the question to focus your attention on the "feeling" of "I am."

Initially, when you ask yourself "Who am I?", your mind will describe you. It may suggest you are your attributes (physical, mental), moralities, and/or actions. Reject these answers. Instead, become one with the question and use it to find the essence of "you" as pure consciousness.

The "you" you seek is the pure existence of one self. There are no concepts, feelings, images, or thoughts attached.

1. Sit in a comfortable position and close your eyes.
2. Take a few deep breaths and mentally scan your body from head to toe. Consciously relax each part.
3. When you're ready, turn your attention to your breath.

4. As you breathe, repeat the mantra "I am." Feel the core meaning of the words absorb into your body. Do not attach any thoughts to the mantra. Just let it circulate within and quiet your mind.

5. Once your mind is still, ask "Who am I?" Look past any tangible answers your mind attempts to provide. Connect to your awareness itself, your sense of being.

6. To begin with, the opening into awareness may only last a few seconds before feelings or thoughts come to surface. When this happens, ask "To whom does this arise?", with the answer being "Me." Then follow-up with the original question, "Who am I?"

7. If needed, you can return to the mantra "I am" to re-center yourself before asking again.

Yoga Nidra

Yoga Nidra (yogic sleep) is conscious relaxation for your whole being.

1. Choose a mantra, affirmation, or visualization to use during the practice.
2. Lie down in a comfortable position and close your eyes.
3. Notice your breathing. Feel your lungs filling with air, your stomach expanding, and then deflating.
4. Imagine a light around your body that expands and contracts as you breathe in and out. Feel the energy coursing through your body.
5. Notice each of your senses, one by one.
6. What sounds do you hear? Near, far, inside, outside.
7. What smells can you smell? Take small sniffs, like a dog does.
8. Taste the air.
9. Feel your body supported on the floor. Which parts of your body are touching?

10. What can you see with your eyes closed? Does the light make shapes on your eyelids?

11. Repeat your mantra mentally three times. Try to feel the way you would if it was true.

12. Mentally scan your body and consciously relax each part. Depending on how long you want to spend, you can be very detailed about this, or only do large areas.

13. Deepen your breath and move your fingers and toes, then your hands and feet.

14. In your own time, stretch your body out in whatever way feels right.

15. Open your eyes when you're ready.

16. Gently hug your knees.

17. Fall to your right side and then gently sit up.

18. Take a moment to reflect on the practice and then go about your day.

There are many free guided Yoga Nidra practices on the internet.

You can search them on YouTube or download them from:

www.YogaNidraNetwork.org/downloads

Related Chapters:

- Breathing
- Visualization

SOUND

In the same way you can focus on your breath or a mantra, you can also meditate on sounds.

From Sound to Silence

For this meditation, you'll need something that will vibrate sound into silence, such as a reverberating bell, a gong, or a glass of water that you tap with a teaspoon.

1. Sit or lie in a comfortable position and take a few deep breaths to calm your mind.
2. Close your eyes and focus your attention on the surrounding sounds.
3. Hit your gong (or whatever you have). It's good to have someone else do it for you, or to get an automated app on your phone.
4. Listen intently to the sound of the gong, all the way until it goes into total silence.
5. Now hear the silence for a little while.
6. When you're ready, hit the gong again.

Hum Pranayama

Here is a simple yoga breathing meditation that incorporates sound.

1. Sit or lie down in a comfortable position. Your mouth should be closed, but your top and bottom teeth shouldn't touch each other.
2. Place your thumbs in your ears.
3. Breath slowly in and out through your nose.
4. As you exhale, make a "huummmm" sound. It should be one long, smooth sound.

5. Feel the vibrations of the sound though your head and upper body.
6. When you're ready to finish the meditation, stop humming and take a minute or two to notice your natural flow of breath.
7. Notice the calming effects the humming has on your mind and body.

Instrumental Stories

1. Prepare a piece of instrumental music. Nothing with lyrics, and nothing from a movie soundtrack that you're familiar with.
2. Sit or lie in a comfortable position, take a few deep breaths, and play the music.
3. Listen to it carefully and as you listen, really feel the music.
4. Construct in your imagination the story the music is telling.
5. If you need a push, the title of the track can spark your imagination.

Music Focus

1. Prepare a piece of instrumental music.
2. Sit or lie in a comfortable position, take a few deep breaths, and play the music.
3. Pick out one instrument in the music and focus on it. Follow only the sound of that one instrument.

Nada Yoga

1. Sit or lie in a comfortable position and close your eyes.
2. Take a few deep breaths to relax your mind and body.
3. When you're ready, turn your attention to the surrounding

sounds. They can be out in the general environment, or some
ambient music of your choice.

4. Focus all your attention on hearing.
5. Next, hear the sounds within your body and mind. This will
   take some practice.
6. Eventually, you will tune in to para nada (the ultimate
   sound). It is the sound of the universe, which has no
   vibration. You may hear it as "om."

Open Hearing

1. Sit or lie in a comfortable position and take a few deep
   breaths to calm your mind.
2. Close your eyes and imagine your ears are as big as your
   body and that they can hear everything.
3. Listen to the sounds near you.
4. Choose one sound and focus on it. Don't label it, just let it be
   a sound. It is neither good nor bad.
5. When you're ready, move onto the next sound, and then the
   next.
6. Next, expand your awareness to hear sounds far away.
7. Listen to sounds as far away as you can.
8. Now turn your attention to your breath. Listen to it intently.

Playing an Instrument

Learning to play an instrument is a great way to meditate because it
requires your complete attention. Once you become better at it, it's
much more than just playing the notes. You connect with the music
and it moves your ego aside. The music flows through you.

VIPASSANA

According to the Buddha, to achieve happiness, you only need to see your true nature, as opposed to relying on external forces like social status or money. The way to do this is with vipassana, which literally means "insight meditation." It relies on your own effort. There is no calling for the help of God or any other external force.

Buddhism identifies desire and ignorance as the roots of suffering. Over time, insight meditation eliminates attachment in the mind, which gradually leads to desire and ignorance being melted away.

Eventually, you may reach the state of "nirvana, "which is a state of freedom from suffering and rebirth, though this definition differs depending on which Buddhist tradition you follow.

The main idea of vipassana is to stay in the now. A good tip for observing body movement is to focus on the movement itself as opposed to the physical body part.

When doing vipassana meditation, use the half-lotus sitting posture.

- Cross your legs so your right foot rests on your left thigh.
- Place the back of your right hand on your left palm.

- Rest your hands in your lap, palms facing the sky.
- Don't slump, but don't be stiff either. Harness the feeling of being relaxed but alert.
- If you use a cushion, ensure your legs are still on the floor.

Note: The half-lotus isn't the only vipassana sitting position, but it is the most common.

Paying Respect to the Teachings

At the start of each meditation session, Buddhists pay respect with this sequence of movements. Even if you are not Buddhist, you can do this as a meditation.

1. Place your hands on your knees, palms facing down.
2. Slowly rotate your right hand so it rests on the edge of your little finger. Your fingers should be together, straight and relaxed.
3. Stop for a moment.
4. Lift your hand straight up about 20 centimeters.
5. Stop for a moment.
6. Move your hand to the front of your chest, so it makes the right half of the prayer hands.
7. Stop for a moment.
8. Now do steps 2 to 7 with your left hand. Your palms should come together in the prayer position, fingers pointing to the sky.
9. Stop for a moment.
10. Gently press your palms together.
11. Stop for a moment.
12. Bow your head a little and mentally say "May I pay respect to the Buddha (wisdom), the Dhamma (ultimate reality), and the Sangha (the company of enlightened beings)."
13. Stop for a moment.

14. Do steps 2 to 12 in reverse order, so you finish in the starting position.

Sitting

This is good to do for a few minutes before the rising-falling meditation. The more advanced you become, the longer you can do it for.

1. Sit in the half lotus.
2. Focus on the feel of the sitting posture and label it "sitting." "Look" with your mind's eye to see how the posture feels in each area, such as your hands or your contact points with the floor, but don't individualize the areas. Look at the whole thing as one.
3. Focus and label it, then focus and label it again. Each focus takes only a few seconds, or about one breath, and the focusing and labeling are simultaneous. Do not focus on the label.
4. Understand that "sitting" is only a momentary group of constantly changing sensations.

Rising-Falling

1. Sit or lie down in a comfortable position.
2. Mentally focus on your abdomen, 3–5 centimeters above your navel. Find where it appears clearest in your mind. When you inhale, your abdomen rises, and when you exhale it falls.
3. Mentally observe the motion of your abdomen rising from start to finish. If you find it difficult to begin with, you can place your hand on your stomach to feel it.
4. Do the same as it falls. It is not one movement. It rises, stops, then falls, and stops before rising again.
5. Do not visualize your abdomen, think about your breathing,

or anything else. Only be mindful of the movement. You can use the labels "rising," "stop," and "falling."

Sitting-Touching

In this practice, the focus of your attention switches between two things.

The first thing is a point on either your left or right buttock where you feel your contact with the floor. Connect your mind to this point. We will call this state of your mind touching it the "contact point."

The second is your sitting posture itself.

1. Adopt the half lotus.
2. Observe the sitting posture. If you need a focal point, use your hands on your lap.
3. Now move your attention to the mental contact point (as opposed to the physical).
4. Alternate your focus between these two things from moment to moment. You can use the labels "sitting" and "touching." Each moment should last as long as it does to say the mental label.
5. The next time you practice this, use the alternate buttock for the contact point.

Rising-Falling-Sitting

Once you notice a pronounced gap between the rising and falling movements in the Rising-Falling exercise, you can add sitting if you wish.

1. Sit in half lotus.
2. Start with the Rising-Falling practice.
3. When you're ready, add in a focus on sitting after falling and before rising. Do this by taking a mental picture of the pose.

4. Now you have three moments of focus: rising, falling, and sitting. No moment should be longer than a few seconds. After practice, all the moments will take equal lengths of time.
5. You can use the mental labels "rising," "falling," and "sitting."

Rising-Falling-Sitting-Touching

In this practice, you add a moment of touching to your meditation.

1. Sit in one of the vipassana postures.
2. Start with the Rising-Falling- Sitting practice.
3. When you are ready, add in a focus on touching after sitting and before rising.
4. Now you have four moments of focus: rising, falling, sitting, and touching. No moment should be longer than a few seconds. After practice, all the moments will take equal lengths of time.
5. You can use the mental labels "rising," "falling," "sitting," and "touching."

Vipassana Walking Meditation

This walking meditation is a slow, deliberate walk. It's best to do it barefoot.

Focus your attention on each action, primarily on each foot moving through the air. Don't look at your feet, but maintain an awareness of them in your mind.

If you are using walking meditation as a break from your sitting meditation (so from sitting to standing), make mindful movements to go from sitting to standing.

1. Find a place where you can walk at least seven steps in a straight line.

2. Look straight ahead or at the floor in front of you. Don't bend your head forward.

3. Stand quiet and gently hold one of your wrists with the other hand in front of your body.

4. Note "standing" for a moment.

5. Next, note "intending to walk."

6. Take one slow, fluid step with your right foot. Be attentive to the entire arc of movement.

7. Label the step "placing" as your foot finds the floor. Wait in this position for a second.

8. Next, take a slow step with your left foot.

9. Repeat this process of slowly stepping with one foot at a time while labeling your movements.

10. At the end of the path take a final step that places your feet together. Note "stopping."

11. Note "standing" for a moment, then "intending to turn."

12. Your turn should happen in four steps. Lift the toes of your right foot and pivot 90° to your right on your heel. Note "turning."

13. As you turn, keep your left foot still and your head in line with your torso.

14. Stop for a second.

15. Now lift your left foot and place it next to your right foot. Note "turning." Stop for a second.

16. Pivot on your right heel another 90°, while noting "turning." Stop.

17. Lift your left foot and place it next to your right foot. Note "turning."

18. Repeat steps 1 to 4.

Progressive Walking Meditation

You can learn advanced walking meditation techniques in the same progressive manner you go from the Rising-Falling meditation to Rising-Falling-Sitting-Touching.

Two-Part Step (Lifting and Placing):

1. Lift your heel, but keep your toes on the floor. Note "lifting."
2. Stop for a moment.
3. Now move the whole foot forward and place it on the floor. Note "placing" as you do it.

Three-Part Step (Lifting, Moving, and Placing):

1. Lift your entire foot straight up. Note "lifting."
2. Stop for a moment.
3. Move your foot forward and note "moving."
4. Stop for a moment.
5. Place your whole foot on the floor. Note "placing" as you do it.

Four-Part Step (Heel up, Lifting, Moving, and Placing):

1. Lift your heel, but keep your toes on the floor. Note "heel up."
2. Stop for a moment.
3. Lift your entire foot straight up. Note "lifting."
4. Stop for a moment.
5. Move your foot forward and note "moving."
6. Stop for a moment.
7. Place your whole foot on the floor. Note "placing" as you do it.

Five-Part Step (Heel up, Lifting, Moving, Lowering, and Placing):

1. Lift your heel with your toes remaining on the floor. Note "heel up."
2. Stop for a moment.
3. Lift your entire foot straight up. Note "lifting."
4. Stop for a moment.

5. Move your foot forward and note "moving."
6. Stop for a moment.
7. Lower your whole foot until it's just off the ground. Note "lowering."
8. Stop for a moment.
9. Place your whole foot on the floor. Note "placing" as you do it.

Six-Part Step (Heel up, Lifting, Moving, Lowering, Touching, and Placing):

1. Lift your heel, but keep your toes remaining on the floor. Note "heel up."
2. Stop for a moment.
3. Lift your entire foot straight up. Note "lifting."
4. Stop for a moment.
5. Move your foot forward and note "moving."
6. Stop for a moment.
7. Lower your whole foot until it's just off the ground. Note "lowering."
8. Stop for a moment.
9. Touch your toes to the floor and nothing else. Note "touching."
10. Stop for a moment.
11. Lower your heel so your whole foot is on the floor. Note "placing" as you do it.

Hand Motions One

This is a good alternative if you can't do the walking meditation because of a disability or other factor. It's also good to do if your mind is wandering during a different meditation.

There's no need to look at your hand while you're doing this practice. Watch the movement with your mind.

1. Sit in half lotus or lie down.
2. If you're sitting, place your hands on your knees, palms down. If you're lying down, place your hands at your sides, palms on the floor.
3. Slowly rotate your right hand to the right so it rests on the edge of your little finger. Your fingers should be together, straight and relaxed. Mentally note "turning."
4. Stop for a moment.
5. Lift your hand up off your knee about 20 centimeters. Mentally note "raising."
6. Stop for a moment.
7. Lower your hand again. Stop when it's about 4 centimeters above your knee. Mentally note "lowering."
8. Continue to move your hand until the edge of it rests back on your knee. Mentally note "touching."
9. Stop for a moment.
10. Rotate your hand to the left until it rests back in its starting position. Mentally note "raising."
11. Repeat steps 3–10 with the same hand for half the time you intend to practice.
12. When you're ready, follow the same process with your left hand.

Hand Motions Two

1. Sit in half lotus or lie down.
2. If you're sitting, place your hands on your knees, palms down. If you're lying down, place your hands at your sides, palms on the floor.
3. Slowly rotate your right hand to the right so it rests on the edge of your little finger. Your fingers should be together, straight and relaxed.
4. Stop for a moment.
5. Lift your right hand up off your knee about 15 centimeters.

6. Stop for a moment.
7. Using your elbow as a pivot point, swing your lower arm toward the center of your body. Your hand, wrist, and forearm should be in a straight line as you move.
8. Stop about 5 centimeters from your abdomen. Your palm should face your stomach, and your fingers should point to your left side.
9. Slowly rotate your left hand to the left, so it rests on the edge of your little finger. Your fingers should be together, straight and relaxed.
10. Stop for a moment.
11. Lift your left hand up off your knee about 15 centimeters.
12. Stop for a moment.
13. Move your left lower arm in toward your abdomen in the same way as you did with your right, until your left hand is touching your right.
14. Stop for a moment.
15. Now do steps 3 to 14 in reverse order, so you finish in your starting position.

You can use labels as you did in the Hand Motions One practice.

Vipassana Mindful Eating

This exercise is a more "detailed" version of mindful eating. When doing this, be sure to allow yourself plenty of time for the meal. One to two hours is sufficient.

As with most of the exercises in this section, you label/note each action before you do it, and pause for a moment between each action.

1. Sit with your food in front of you, palms facing down and resting on your knees.
2. Look at your food.
3. Notice your state of hunger, or lack thereof.

4. Turn one of your hands until it rests on its pinky side.
5. Lift that same hand up to table height.
6. Move the hand forward toward your utensil.
7. Take hold of the utensil while you focus your awareness on the feeling of touch.
8. Raise the utensil.
9. Move the utensil to your food.
10. Get some food with the utensil.
11. Lift the food to your mouth.
12. Touch the food to your mouth. Notice the feeling of it.
13. Open your mouth.
14. Put the food in your mouth.
15. Close your mouth and notice the sensation and taste of the food in your mouth. Don't chew yet.
16. Lower your hand.
17. Put the utensil on your plate.
18. Place your hand back on your knee, palm facing down.
19. Chew the food. Notice the movement of your mouth and the individual flavors.
20. When you're ready, swallow the food. Feel it moving down your throat.
21. Notice your empty mouth.
22. Notice your state of hunger, or lack thereof.
23. Repeat steps 4 to 22.
24. If you take a drink, apply the same method of mindfulness.

Note: If you need to use both hands to cut your food, only focus on one hand.

Related Chapters:

- Breathing
- Mindfulness

VISUALIZATION

Visualization in meditation is when you focus on a mental image. By using it to engage your mind, you can experience the impact of that visualization on your mind and body.

Blackboard Drawing

1. Write out an affirmation or goal you want to meditate on.
2. Sit or lie down in a comfortable position, with your eyes closed.
3. Take a few deep breaths to center yourself.
4. When you're ready, imagine a blackboard.
5. Think of your chosen affirmation or goal in writing on the blackboard.
6. Imagine yourself drawing a visual representation of those words. Be creative. The more time you have to meditate, the more detailed you can make your drawing.
7. Once your drawing is complete, capture the essence of it in your feelings, so you're "living" the affirmation or goal.

Breathing Colors

1. Sit, lie, or stand in a comfortable position.
2. Close your eyes and notice your breath.
3. Imagine inhaling the color gold. It fills your entire body with everything positive—love, happiness, calm, etc.
4. Exhale the color gray. With it goes all negative emotion—hate, fear, jealousy, anxiety, etc.

Exploring Outer Space

1. Lie down in a comfortable position, with your eyes closed.
2. Take a few deep breaths to calm your mind and relax your body.
3. With each exhalation, imagine your body becoming lighter and lighter, until it floats.
4. Visualize yourself floating higher and higher—above the trees and buildings, through the clouds and into outer space. You can visit another planet if you wish.
5. Enjoy the feeling of being light and free in both mind and body.
6. When you're ready, allow yourself to float down to earth and all the way back into the room you're in.
7. When you sense that your body is grounded again, slowly move your fingers and toes.
8. Finally, move larger portions of your body and continue with your day.

Level of Light

This is a good meditation to release stress from your body. You can do it even if you have only a few minutes to spare.

1. Stand or lie in a comfortable position.
2. Take a few deep breaths to calm your mind and relax your body.
3. Continue to breathe deeply. With each exhale, visualize a level of light gathering all your tension as it moves down your body.
4. With each breath, imagine that the level of light gets lower and lower, gathering all the stress and negativity, until it dissipates out through your feet.
5. Cover a section of your body with each breath: your head,

arms, torso, mid-section, legs, and your feet. This is only six breaths. You can make it more or fewer breaths/sections depending on how much time you have.

6. When you're done, take a moment to feel the aftereffects of the practice before continuing with your day.

Mental Picture

1. Find a picture (photo, art, etc.) or object you like and put in in front of you.
2. Spend one minute looking at it. Observe all the details.
3. Now close your eyes and visualize the picture or object in your mind. Try to remember the little details.
4. When you're ready, open your eyes and look at the object for another minute.
5. Close your eyes and visualize it again with the new details you've just seen.

Mountain Stillness

1. Stand relaxed and close your eyes.
2. Take a few deep breaths to calm your mind.
3. Feel your whole body—its position, size, weight, etc.
4. Imagine your body is a mountain, big, heavy, and stable.
5. With each exhale, visualize your body transforming into a mountain.
6. Once you're a complete mountain, feel yourself getting more relaxed and rooted into the ground with each exhale.
7. When you're ready, transform back to your normal state. With each inhalation, become more like your normal self.

Third-Eye Meditation

In this simple meditation, you focus your attention on your third eye, which is the spot between your eyebrows.

1. Sit or lie in a comfortable position and close your eyes.
2. Focus your attention on your third eye.
3. Whenever your mind wanders, acknowledge the thought and return your attention to your third eye.
4. With practice, you will focus on your third eye for longer periods without having distracting thoughts entering your mind.

MANTRAS

A mantra is a word or phrase you can use to focus your mind into a meditative state. Some of them have special literal meanings, while others are more valuable for the sound they produce. There are various ways to use mantras in meditation. For example, they can be:

- Recited
- Listened to
- Used with other meditative methods such as breathing or chakras
- Combined with any of the above

There is a traditional progression when you're reciting a mantra:

- Out loud
- Whispering
- Mental only

After some time, you will reach "ajapa japa," or spontaneous listening. This is when you no longer need to repeat the mantra, but it will continue on its own in your mind, all the time.

General Tips for Mantra Meditation

- For a formal practice, sit in a comfortable position with your eyes closed.
- Informally, you can repeat a mantra in the back of your mind. In this way, it doesn't matter if your eyes are open or even if you're doing other simple tasks.
- Repeat your mantra at a speed of your choice, or as instructed, depending on the specific meditation.
- A fast repetition produces gamma waves in your brain, which will energize you. A slow repetition produces theta waves and will calm your mind.
- The speed is up to you and depends on what you want from the practice, but you shouldn't continuously swap speeds during the same practice.
- Maintain a continuous and relaxed awareness of each repetition of the mantra.
- If you lose focus because you have a busy mind, vocalize your mantra louder. As your minds quiets, so will your mantra.

Related Chapters:

- Breathing

BUDDHIST MANTRAS

Mantra meditation is common in Buddhism. Here is a list of various mantras you can try:

Chinese Mantras

- Namo Amituofo

Nichiren Buddhist Mantra

- Nam Myōhō Renge Kyō

Pali Mantras

- Buddho
- Buddham saranam gacchami. Dhammam saranam gacchami. Sangham saranam gacchami.
- Om shanti shanti shanti
- Sabbe satta sukhi hontu

Sanskrit Mantras

- Gate gate paragate parasamgate bodhi svaha
- Om Mani Padme Hum
- Om Tare Tuttare Ture Svaha

CHAKRA MANTRA

According to Hindu belief, chakras are the seven energy centers of our bodies. They are internal and run vertically from the base of the spine to the top of the head. Our "kundalini" (life force, qi, energy, prana) travels up though these chakras.

The five lower chakras connect us with each of the five basic elements of the universe.

The two higher chakras are the third eye and the crown.

The third eye contains "maha tatva," which is the supreme element and the source of all other elements. The crown chakra is beyond all elements.

Important: Never "play" with the kundalini. Awakening it requires professional guidance, and if that's done without care, bad things can happen.

Mantra meditation is a good way to balance your chakras without the risk.

Do it by repeating the "bija mantras" related to the five lower chakras. Start at the base and work your way up.

1. Sit or lie down in a comfortable position and take a few deep breaths.
2. Start by focusing on where your base chakra is in your body, and repeat the mantra "lam" three times.
3. Next, do your sacral chakra, repeating the mantra "vam" three times.
4. Continue in this manner though the rest of your chakras.
5. After completing the chakra mantras, recite any other mantra of your choice.
6. Repeat steps 2 to 5 two more times (three times in total).

7. Stop the cycle at seven chakra mantras, and only chant your chosen mantra until the end of your practice.

Here are the 7 bija mantras with their mantras, pronunciations in parentheses, colors, and elements:

1. Crown - silence - violet - vibrations
2. Third eye - om (aum) - indigo - light
3. Throat - ham (hum) - blue - ether/space
4. Heart - yam (yum) - green - air
5. Solar plexus - ram (rum) - yellow - fire
6. Sacral - vam (vum) - orange - water
7. Base - lam (lum) - red - earth

If you need guidance on the pronunciation of the mantras, you can check out this YouTube video:

https://youtu.be/Phıcff2AITc

Chakra Mantra Dharana

In this variation, all you do is repeat your favorite mantra. While you do so, focus on either your third eye chakra or your heart chakra. Allow your mantra to originate from the chakra you are focusing on.

Chakra Single Mantra

Each chakra has a color. Choose one chakra and repeat its mantra as you visualize its color (see chakra mantra). End the practice by repeating "om" to balance your kundalini.

OM MANTRA

The "om" mantra (AUM) is more than a mere sound. The vibrations created in the sounds and the meaning behind them are deep.

If you use the "om" mantra without care for its meaning, you will have a pleasant and balanced feeling. But if you use the "om" mantra with a sense of its deeper meanings, you will have a much richer experience.

There are seven meanings and methods of the "om" mantra.

With experimentation, you may find one that feels best to you. Stick with that one for a while. In time, the others will come, and they will merge into one experience.

1. Pulsing repetition
2. With the flow of breath
3. As the object called universe
4. Sound vibration of the universe
5. Gross, subtle, and causal planes
6. Waking, dreaming, and deep sleep consciousness
7. Conscious, unconscious, subconscious mind

Pulsing Repetition

In this om meditation you will realize the many rhythms within your mind and body.

1. Imagine the sound of "om," rising and falling at a speed natural for you.
2. Experiment with different speeds, such as:

- OmmOmmOmm...
- OmmmmOmmmmOmmmm...

- OmmmmmmmOmmmmmmmOmmmmmmm...

With the Flow of Breath

In this meditation, make no sound. Chant "om" only in your mind and let it flow with your breath. In this way, you will experience your mind, breath, and the mantra as one.

You can chant on each part of the breath:

- Exhale: Om
- Inhale: Om

or only on exhalation:

- Inhale: (silence)
- Exhale: Om

There is no pause between each breath.

You will find the speed of the mantra will naturally slow. This is good, but don't force it. Allow it to happen naturally while you keep your mind alert and sink deeper into meditation.

As the Object Called Universe

Your mind naturally associates words with meaning and objects. For example, when someone says "cloud," you may imagine a fluffy ball of white.

The object of "om" is the one-ness of the entire universe. Not each item that makes up the universe, but the universe as a whole.

When you chant "om," expand your awareness to encompass the one-ness of the universe. Know that this one word contains the whole universe.

This may be difficult at the start. The universe is massive, and it is daunting to fit it into a single word. Continue to chant "om," and with each chant, expand your awareness. Incorporate more and more of the universe into the word, until "om" is the universe.

Sound Vibration of the Universe

The subtle sound of "om" is a constant vibration in the universe, and is the base vibration from which all other vibrations come from. You may hear it naturally as a constant ring or buzzing sound when your surroundings are silent. Deep yoga meditation will also tune you into it, and the deeper you get, the louder will get.

To evoke the sound of "om," repeat the "om" mantra as you visualize the underlying vibration of the universe.

And as you listen to the vibration of "om," know that you are listening to the vibration of the universe. After some practice, you will hear it as the deeper sound of "om."

While listening for "om," do not suppress your thoughts and emotions. Instead, let them pass through you.

Gross, Subtle, and Causal Planes

The "om" mantra has four parts, and each part has a meaning.

- A. The gross (physical) world.
- U. The subtle (astral/intuitive) realm.
- M. The causal plane (background stillness) from which the gross and subtle emerge, and where they rest when inactive. It is akin to the blank canvas of a painting, where the gross and subtle are the paints.
- **Silence**. The absolute reality which is the foundation of the other three parts.

Chant the "om" mantra slowly, so you have time to gain awareness of each level while keeping a continuous sound. For example, chant:

AaaaaaUuuuuuMmmmmm (Silence)...

Contemplate the meaning of each part as you chant it. With practice, the chant will quicken and the silence will be longer. You will also grasp the concept of each part more deeply.

Waking, Dreaming, and Deep Sleep

The four parts of "om" are connected to the four states of consciousness.

- **A - Waking.** Being aware of being awake. You become aware of your mental and emotional processes.
- **U - Dreaming.** Not having a dream, but being mindful of the dream state beneath the waking state.
- **M - Sleep.** Being aware of the complete stillness of your mind when you're in deep sleep with no active thought processes.
- **Silence.** Observing the other three states of conscious "om." You are a witness to waking, dreaming, and deep sleep.

The states of deep sleep, samadhi (meditative consciousness), and death function at the same levels.

This meditation is very personal, because you become conscious of internal states. Ultimately, these states and the external states from the previous mediation will merge into one awareness.

Conscious, Unconscious, Subconscious Mind

The four parts of "om" are connected to the four levels (not states) of consciousness.

- **A - Conscious.** What your mind knows of in the physical world, such as reading.
- **U - Subconscious.** Where your mind functions at an "automatic" level that you need not actively think about, such as when your heart is beating.
- **M - Unconscious.** The place in which your mind stores information that is brought to the conscious mind when needed, such as memories.
- **Silence - Pure consciousness**, which flows though the other three levels of consciousness. It is the state in which all the other levels of the mind are witnessed. At this stage, one is a seer.

SYNCHRONIZED MANTRA AND BREATHING

Here are some examples of how you can synchronize a mantra with different breathing patterns:

A-Ham ("I am")

- Inhale "a," exhale "ham."

So-Ham

- Inhale "so," exhale "ham."
- Focus your attention up and down your spine as you breathe.

Soham - Hamsa

- Inhale "so" through your left nostril.
- Exhale "ham" through your right nostril.
- Inhale "ham" through your right nostril.
- Exhale "sa" through your left nostril.

MISCELLANEOUS MANTRAS

Mahavakyas

Mahavakyas are "great sayings" from Vedanta mantra meditation. As you repeat each mantra, contemplate the meaning of it. Some examples of mahavakyas are:

- Aham Brahmasmi ("I am Brahman")
- Sarvam khalvidam brahman ("All is Brahman")
- Tat Vam Asi ("Thou art That")

Mantra Japa

Mantra Japa is part of Bhakti yoga, which is the "yoga of devotion."

Repeat the name (or a short prayer containing that name) of the Divine in the way you prefer. Induce a feeling of devotion to recite it.

The mantra you recite depends on the deity. Here are a few examples. The deity is on the left, with the corresponding mantra on the right.

- Ganesh: Om Gam Ganapataye Namaha
- Saraswati: Om Aim Mahasarasvatyai Namah
- Shiva: Om Namah Shivaya
- Vishnu: Om Namo Bhagavate Vasudevaya

Mantra Writing

1. Sit in a quiet and comfortable place where you can write without distraction.
2. Choose a mantra and continuously write it out.
3. As you write the mantra, fix your eyes on the words and recite them either out aloud, in a whisper, or mentally.

4. When you're ready, write the mantra out again in print as small and as neat as you can make it. This will intensify the exercise.

So Hum

This simple mantra meditation is a good way to experience "being."

1. Sit in a comfortable position with your hands in your laps.
2. Scan your body from head to toe and consciously relax each body part.
3. Bring your awareness to your breath.
4. As you inhale, repeat "so" to yourself.
5. On your exhale, say "hum" to yourself.
6. When you are comfortable that the so-hum is coordinated with your breath, contemplate the meaning of the mantra.
7. If thoughts arise, come back to the mantra: "so hum."

Inhale: So (I am). Become one with your inner being of self. Consider the source of your breath and how everything is connected to the same universal rhythm.

Exhale: Hum (all that is). Your exhale releases you as energy into the universe. Visualize it flowing out to connect with the universe, with the "all that is."

MUDRAS

A mudra is a symbolic body gesture found in a variety of disciplines. It helps to focus the mind, increase awareness, and stimulate energy flow through your body.

In Buddhism mudras have spiritual meaning, whilst in Ayurveda or Jin Shin Jyutsu, you can use them for healing.

There are hundreds of mudras. In this book, you will learn some of the most common hand mudras in Buddhism, yoga, and Jin Shin Jyutsu.

Here is a generic method for meditating with mudras.

1. Sit or lie down in a comfortable position.
2. Take a few breaths to center yourself.
3. When you're ready, place your hands in the position of the mudra.
4. Hold the mudra while engaging in mindful breathing or another meditation of your choice.

5. If you chose a mudra for its specific meaning or use, you can meditate on that.

Related Chapters:

- Buddhist Mudras
- Jin Shin Jyutsu Mudras
- Yoga Mudras

BUDDHIST MUDRAS

Note: See the Daoist chapter for an explanation of the dantian.

Abhaya

The abhaya mudra takes its characteristics from Buddha Shakyamuni and Dhyani Buddha Amoghasiddhi. It embodies benevolence, peace, protection, and shedding fear.

1. Raise your right hand with your fingertips at shoulder height.
2. Your right arm should be bent at the elbow, with your fingers upright together and your palm facing out.
3. Your left hand should rest in front of your lower dantian, palm facing up.

Anjali

In Buddhism, this classic mudra represents adoration, greeting, and prayer. With it you lift your heart center towards your hands. Other names for this mudra are "namaskara" and "hridayanjali."

This is also a yoga mudra. In yoga, it expresses gratitude and respect.

1. Gently press the palms of your hands together.
2. Hold them so your thumbs rest against your sternum.

Bhumisparsa

Bhumisparsa is the mudra of "touching the earth." It represents the awakening of Buddha.

1. Hold your right hand is above your right knee with your palm facing toward you.
2. Let your fingers hang gently down.
3. Rest your left hand in front of your lower dantian, palm facing up.

Dharmachakra

This mudra is the "teaching of the wheel of dharma." It depicts Buddha's first sermon in Sarnath after he attained enlightenment.

1. Hold both your hands in front of your chest, with the tips of your forefingers touching the tips of the thumbs on the same hand.
2. Your left hand should face in and your right hand should face out.
3. Your left hand should be in front of your right.

Dhyana

Dhyana is the mudra of meditation. It will deepen your mind and bring inner peace. In this mudra, you right hand represents enlightenment, and your left represents illusion.

Other names for this are the samadhi mudra and the yoga mudra.

1. Place your hands on your lap, right hand on top and palms facing up.
2. The tips of your thumbs touch each other.

Karana

This mudra wards off evil and negative feelings such as fear, hate, and self-pity. Since it sheds negative feelings, it also reduces sickness.

1. Place the tip of your thumb over the tip of your middle finger.
2. Straighten your index and little finger.
3. Allow your ring finger to rest curl close to your middle finger.

Uttarabodhi

The uttarabohi mudra connects you to the universe and helps you to attain supreme enlightenment.

1. Touch your index fingers together and point them to the sky.
2. Interlock the rest of your fingers.
3. Place your hands at your heart.

Vajra

This symbolizes the five elements (earth, air, fire, water, and metal).

1. With your left hand in a loose fist, point your index finger to the sky.
2. Grasp this finger with your right hand.
3. Join the tips of your right thumb, right index finger, and left index finger.
4. Hold the mudra in front of your heart.

Varada

This is the mudra of giving and other things such as charity, compassion, sincerity, and welcome.

1. Hold your right hand in front of your right knee, fingers pointing down and palm facing out.
2. Your left hand should be open, palm facing up, and resting at your lower dantian.

Vitarka

Vitarka signifies the sharing of Buddhist teachings.

1. With your right hand, touch the tips of your thumb and index finger together. The rest of your fingers will curl naturally.

2. Hold your right hand at your heart.
3. Your left hand should rest in front of your lower dantian, palm facing up.

Related Chapters:

- Daoist
- Yoga Mudras

JIN SHIN JYUTSU MUDRAS

The exploration of ancient hand mudras is how the rediscovery of Jin Shin Jyutsu (JSJ) began. From them come the eight most powerful Jin Shin Jyutsu hand mudras to practice.

Place your hands in the positions described below. Hold each mudra for two minutes, or until you feel your pulses align and/or you feel a sense of calmness.

Each JSJ mudra has specific benefits. Often you will feel an urge to stay in one particular mudra for longer. This means you have problems that you need to fix in that area. That's fine. Stay with that mudra for as long as you wish.

When doing these hand mudras, keep your hands, arms, and shoulders as relaxed as possible. Don't grip your fingers tight. Hold them loosely.

Exhaling the Burdens and Blockages

Use this mudra to release general stress from your whole being.

1. Hold your left middle finger with your right hand.
2. Place your thumb on the palm and the rest of your fingers on the back of the hand.
3. Repeat this with opposite hands.

Inhaling the Abundance

This mudra opens your ability to inhale qi.

1. Hold your left middle finger with your right hand.
2. Place your thumb is on the back of the finger and the rest of your fingers on the palm side.
3. Repeat this with opposite hands.

Calm and Revitalize

This is a good mudra to use when you're depressed, nervous, or have a worry in your heart. It calms your body and releases tension which revitalizing the body organs.

1. Hold your left little and ring fingers with your right hand.
2. Place your thumb on the palm side of these fingers and the rest of your fingers are on the back.
3. Repeat this with opposite hands.

Releasing General Daily Fatigue

With this mudra, you will feel the release of fatigue, stress, and tension which builds up during the day. Negative feelings such as anger, fear, and worry will disappear.

1. Hold your left thumb, index, and middle fingers with your right hand.
2. Place your thumb on the back and the rest of your fingers on the palm side.
3. Repeat this with opposite hands.

Total Revitalization

This mudra will revitalize all your bodily functions. It is great for combatting daily fatigue.

1. Make a circle with your right thumb and right middle finger.
2. Place the pad of your thumb over the fingernail of your finger.
3. Place your left thumb in between your right middle finger and right thumb.
4. Repeat this with opposite hands.

Breathing Easily

Use this mudra to strengthen your respiratory function. Do it while exercising to help you breathe easier.

1. Touch the palm side of your right thumb and ring fingernail.
2. Repeat this with opposite hands or do both hands at the same time.

Exhaling Dirt, Dust, and Greasy Grime

This releases daily tension and stress. It also harmonizes your mind and body.

1. Touch the palm sides of your middle fingers together.
2. Interlock the rest of your fingers.

Inhaling the Purified Breath of Life

Use this last mudra to harmonize your mind and body.

1. Touch the fingernails of your middle fingers together.

YOGA MUDRAS

Adi

Use this mudra to increase the flow of oxygen in your body. It will relax your nervous system and reduce snoring.

1. With both hands, make a loose fist around your thumb.
2. Rest your fists on your thighs, palms facing the sky.

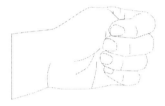

Apan Vayu

Apan vayu is good for pain relief and cardiac disease. Another name for this mudra is "mritasanjeevani."

1. With both hands, curl your middle and ring fingers towards your palm.
2. Place your thumb over the fingertips of these two fingers.
3. Pass your index finger under these fingers to rest on your palm.
4. Keep your little finger straight.
5. Rest your hands on your thighs, palms facing the sky.

Apana

The apana mudra is good for digestion. It eliminates waste from the body and negativity from the mind.

1. Curl your middle and ring fingers towards your palm.
2. Place your thumb over the fingertips of these two fingers.
3. Keep your index and little finger straight and relaxed.

Brahma

In Hinduism, Brahma is the god of creation. The brahma mudra symbolizes consciousness. Use it to release negative energy and there-fore reach a higher meditative state.

1. With both hands, make a loose fist around your thumb.
2. Touch your knuckles together and face your palms to the sky.
3. Hold your hands in front of your navel.

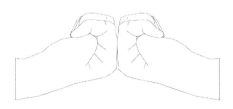

Buddhi

Using this mudra improves mental clarity. It will help you understand messages from your subconscious, such as dreams and visions, and will improve your communication.

1. Touch the tips of your thumb and little finger.
2. Hold all other fingers straight.

Chimaya

Chinmaya is the symbol of pure awareness, and literally means "pure wisdom" in Sanskrit.

It stimulates digestion.

1. With your palms facing the sky, place your right fingers on top of your left.
2. Touch the tips of your thumbs together.
3. Rest your hands on your thighs.

Ganesha

The ganesha mudra takes its name from the Hindu god Ganesh, the remover of obstacles.

Use this mudra to help with obstructions and hard times in your life. It will boost your courage and positivity to help you fight through your burdens. It will also strengthen your heart, both physically and spiritually.

When doing this mudra, focus your prana into your heart chakra (for information on chakras, see the Mantra chapter).

1. Place your hands in front of your chest, right in front of left.
2. Your right palm should face you, thumb on top. Your left should face away from you, thumb on the bottom.
3. Clasp your hands together in a monkey grip.
4. As you meditate with this mudra, inhale deeply. Then as you exhale, pull outward while keeping a grip on your fingers.
5. After six breaths, reverse your hand position, so that your right thumb faces down.
6. Do six more breaths, as before. It is important to do the same number of breaths.
7. You can also use the chant "om gam ganapatayei namaha" on each exhale, which invokes the powers of Ganesh.

Gyan

The gyan mudra improves concentration, creativity, and memory. Use it for gaining insight into your life or a specific issue.

This also has the name chin mudra.

1. Touch the fingertip of your index finger to the tip of your thumb.
2. Keep the rest of your fingers straight and relaxed.
3. Rest your hands on your leg.
4. If you want to feel more grounded, hold your palms facing down. Face them up to feel open and receptive.

Prana

The prana mudra activates the prana (vital energy) in your body. It will invigorate you and give you strength.

1. Hold your fingers together, pointing to the sky.
2. Curl your pinky and ring fingers down and your thumb up.
3. Make sure the tips of these three digits meet in the middle.
4. Keep your other two fingers straight and relaxed.

Rudra

Use the rudra mudra to activate the solar plexus chakra, which is your personal power center (for information on chakras, see the Mantras chapter).

It improves concentration, energizes the physical body, and encourages change to help you reach your goals.

1. Bring the tips of your thumb, index finger and ring finger.
2. Hold your middle and little finger straight and relaxed.

Shuni

The shuni mudra balances your emotions and thoughts and gives you a feeling of stability. It also improves alertness, intuition, and patience.

Another name for this mudra is "shoonya."

1. Touch the tip of your thumb to the tip of your middle finger.
2. Keep your other three fingers straight and relaxed.

Surya

The surya mudra improves digestion and metabolism by activating the fire element in your body. It also improves your immune system and brings positive change.

1. Bend your ring finger down and put your thumb over its second section.
2. Hold the rest of your fingers straight and relaxed.
3. Keep your middle and index fingers together.

Varun

Varun mudra is a symbol of openness, and will improve your communication skills. It increases intuition and mental clarity.

1. Bring together the tips of your little finger and thumb.
2. Keep your other three fingers straight, together, and relaxed.

Vayu

The Vayu mudra is good for any imbalance of air in your body, such as bloating, gas, or stomachache.

1. Fold your index finger down and use your thumb to cover it over to the first knuckle.
2. Press down, but not so much that it's uncomfortable.
3. Hold your other three fingers together. Make them straight and relaxed.

Related Chapters:

- Mantras

RELIGIOUS MEDITATIONS

In this section, sample meditations from two religions are high-lighted, but meditation plays a part in most religions. There are many others, including Buddhist ones, in different sections of this book.

CHRISTIAN

Christian meditation is a way to reflect upon the revelations of God by filling the mind with thoughts related to Christianity, such as Biblical passages. It involves more reflection than common prayer.

Christian Mantra

Choose any sacred word from Christian tradition and recite it with feelings of devotion. Here are some examples of Christian mantras you can use:

- Abba
- Father
- Jesus
- Lord
- Love
- Maranatha (Aramaic for "Come, Lord!")
- Mary
- Mercy

Hesychasm

Hesychasm (the Jesus Prayer) is an Eastern Orthodox tradition dating back to the dawn of Christianity. In Greek, the word "Hesychius" means "silence" or "stillness."

To do Hesychasm, you chant sacred words, such as:

- "O God, make speed to save me. O Lord, make haste to help me."
- "Lord Jesus Christ, Son of God, have mercy on me, a sinner."

1. Choose one of the above sentences to chant.

2. Repeat it while focusing emotional energy into it.
3. Synchronize your chanting with your breath. Inhale: "O God, make speed to save me." Exhale: "O Lord, make haste to help me."
4. After some practice, you'll be able to maintain the prayer during your daily activity.

Lectio Divina

Lectio divina means "divine reading" or "divine word."

1. Choose a short passage from the scripture and memorize it.
2. Repeat it in your mind.
3. As you do this, allow all thoughts related to the passage are surface in your thoughts.

Meditations on the Teachings

There are direct mentions of meditation in the Bible, mostly all in the Book of Psalms.

This meaning of meditation is to think deeply, ponder, and reflect.

1. Read the Bible.
2. As you read, deeply ponder over the meaning of the text.
3. Reflect on its meaning in relation to God.

Modern Contemplative Prayer

This is the Christian meditation created by John Main, an Irish Benedictine monk who learned mantra meditation from a Hindu swami in Malaysia.

1. Choose a sacred word from Christian tradition, such as "Father," "Jesus," "Mary," "Mercy," or "Lord."

2. Continually repeat the word with the same emotion and focus that you put into prayer.
3. When your mind wanders, bring it back to the sacred word.

Sitting with God

In this silent meditation, you focus your whole being—mind, heart, and soul—on God.

1. Start with contemplative prayer or reading to calm your mind.
2. When ready, focus your attention to the greatness and presence of God, so there is a feeling of surrender.
3. Rest in this silent surrender.
4. When any emotions or thoughts arise, offer them to God through your meditation.
5. You can experiment with other points of focus, such as gratitude, love, or themes of Christian life, to see what works best for you.

Related Chapters:

- Mantras

SUFRI

The goal of Sufism is to achieve a mystical union with God (Allah) as you purify yourself.

Yoga influences many Sufi meditations, but it is the remembrance of God which drives it

Awareness of the Heart

This is a Jikr practice—a remembrance of God. Specifically, it is Jikr-e-Sirr or Wakoof Kulbi, or an awareness of the heart.

In Sufi tradition, the spiritual heart is in the same place as the physical heart, a little to the left of the center of your chest.

1. Sit or lie down in a comfortable position. Calm your mind with a few deep breaths.
2. Collect all your external energy and store it within.
3. Focus intensely on the location of your heart until you forget yourself in a state of self-oblivion. This is the path to the Infinite.
4. When ready, do one of the following while focusing on your heart and cultivating a feeling of love for God:

- Listen to your heartbeat
- Repeat the mantra "Allah" (the zikr)
- Focus your attention on God or your spiritual master

Elemental Breath

In this Sufi breathing meditation, there is a focus on the five natural elements.

For each element, do five full breath cycles through your nose at a natural breathing rate.

Earth:

1. Inhale through your nose. Imagine the magnetism and energy of the earth drawing into you. It circulates through your body's energy systems, renewing your vitality.
2. Exhale through your nose. Release all the heavy elements from within you into the ground. Feel lighter, less dense, and revitalized.

Water:

1. Inhale through your nose.
2. Visualize pure energy pouring into you from the heavens. It flows through your body and dissolves any blockages along the way.
3. Exhale through your mouth. Feel purified as the energy stream flows through you.

Fire:

1. Inhale through your mouth. Let the flow of fire breath settle at your solar plexus.
2. Exhale through your nose. The purifying energy of fire rises as it gathers blockages and impurities to your heart. Here, they burn up and are expelled as light out through the crown of your head and between your shoulder blades.

Air:

1. Inhale though your mouth. The element of air blows through the spaces of your whole body, purifying any obstruction or density that remains.

2. Exhale though your mouth.

Ether:

1. Breathe gently through your nostrils.
2. Visualize the element of the ancients (ether) dissolving any remaining sense of density.
3. Open your mind and heart to the vastness of the physical and spiritual realms.

Closing:

Meditate on the renewed feeling you have after these 25 breaths. Carry this feeling with you as you go on with your day.

Nazar Bar Kadam

Nazar bar kadam (watch your step) is the Sufi practice of mindful walking.

1. Walk while contemplating God.
2. Look at your feet so nothing else pollutes your mind as you walk.

Samazen

Samazen is the Sufi method of "whirling."

This is the soul dancing for the love of God. Abandon all ego and merge with love.

1. Put on some trance-like music and whirl in repetitive, clockwise circles.
2. Hold your right hand up to the sky and your left toward the ground.
3. Fix your gaze on your left hand.

Sufi Breathing Meditation

In Sufi breathing practice, you strive to remain in God's presence with every breath.

1. Sit in a comfortable position with your eyes closed.
2. Take a few normal breaths.
3. Focus your attention to your spiritual heart and God.
4. As you inhale, feel the light of God entering your heart as you mentally repeat "Allah."
5. On your exhale, feel the light of "Hu" forcefully striking your heart as you mentally repeat "Hu."
6. Gradually increase your breathing rate while maintaining steps 3 to 5. Take shallow, fast breaths with a longer inhalation and a short, forceful exhalation. Aim for your breathing rate to be three to four times faster than your starting speed.
7. Continue this for 10 minutes.

Zikr

Zikr (also Dhikr or Jikr) means "remembrance," and is the Sufi name for mantra. It is akin to Christian mantras you chant to give devotion to god.

Here are four common Sufi mantras:

- Allah (God)
- Allah hu (God, just He)
- La ilaha illa 'llah (There is no God but God)
- La ilaha illa hu (There is no God but He)

1. Choose your manta.
2. Sit somewhere quiet in a comfortable position.

3. As you inhale, say the first part of the mantra, such as "Aal" or "Allah."
4. On your exhale, say the second part, such as "lah" or "hu."
5. While you repeat the mantra, focus on one of the following:

- The remembrance of God.
- Your solar plexus
- Your spiritual heart.
- The written version of the mantra
- Writing the mantra

Eventually the zikr will continue in your heart at all times, which leads us to the Sufi saying:

"First you do the zikr, and then the zikr does you."

Related Chapters:

- Christian

THANKS FOR READING

Dear reader,

Thank you for reading *The Meditation Workbook.*

If you enjoyed this book, please leave a review where you bought it. It helps more than most people think.

Don't forget your FREE book chapters!

You will also be among the first to know of FREE review copies, discount offers, bonus content, and more.

Go to:

https://offers.SFNonfictionBooks.com/Free-Chapters

Thanks again for your support.

REFERENCES

Bisio, T. (2013). *Decoding the DAO: Nine Lessons in Daoist Meditation: A Complete and Comprehensive Guide to Daoist Meditation*. Outskirts Press.

Burmeister, A. Monte, T. (1997). *The Touch of Healing: Energizing the Body, Mind, and Spirit With Jin Shin Jyutsu*. Bantam.

Cherng, W. (2014). *Daoist Meditation: The Purification of the Heart Method of Meditation and Discourse on Sitting and Forgetting*. Singing Dragon.

Dalai Lama. (2009). *The Art of Happiness: A Handbook for Living*. Hachette.

Dalai Lama. (2018). *An Introduction to Buddhism (Core Teachings of Dalai Lama)*. Shambhala.

Decker, B. (2018). *Practical Meditation for Beginners: 10 Days to a Happier, Calmer You*. Althea Press.

Dienstmann, G. *www.LiveAndDare.com.*

Douglas-Klotz, N. (2005). *The Sufi Book of Life: 99 Pathways of the Heart for the Modern Dervish*. Penguin Books.

Miller, O. (2004). *Essential Yoga: An Illustrated Guide to Over 100 Yoga Poses and Meditations*. Chronicle Books.

Prout, S. (2019). *Dear Universe: 200 Mini-Meditations for Instant Manifestations*. Mariner Books.

Yun, W. (2019). *Climbing the Steps to Qingcheng Mountain: A Practical Guide to the Path of Daoist Meditation and Qigong*. Singing Dragon.

AUTHOR RECOMMENDATIONS

Discover How to Use Yoga as Medicine

Add this book to your collection, because with it you can use yoga to heal
your mind, body, and spirit.

Get it now.

www.SFNonfictionBooks.com/Curing-Yoga

Discover 80+ Sustainable Living Projects

Start making your home more sustainable today, because this book has DIY projects for everyone!

Get it now.

www.SFNonfictionBooks.com/DIY-Sustainable-Home-Projects

ABOUT AVENTURAS

Aventuras has three passions: travel, writing, and self-improvement. She is also blessed (or cursed) with an insatiable thirst for general knowledge.

Combining these things, Miss Viaje spends her time exploring the world and learning. She takes what she discovers and shares it through her books.

www.SFNonfictionBooks.com

amazon.com/author/aventuras

goodreads.com/AventurasDeViaje

facebook.com/AuthorAventuras

instagram.com/AuthorAventuras

Printed in Great Britain
by Amazon

81163440R00079